Bishop Auckland

The growth of a historic market town

Historic England

Bishop Auckland

The growth of a historic market town

Clare Howard and Jayne Rimmer with Jules Brown

Front cover: Bishop Auckland's core
is a mixture of old and new. Its
variety of building materials gives
the town its colourful and attractive
appearance. [DP290640, Alun Bull
© Historic England Archive]

Inside front cover: The town centre
of Bishop Auckland including
Auckland Castle and Park. [Sharon
Soutar © Historic England]

Frontispiece: Fore Bondgate has a
range of smaller independent shops
and provides a flavour of the older
character of the town. [DP290684,
Alun Bull © Historic England
Archive]

Acknowledgements: Surviving
classical-style terracotta doorcase in
Newgate Street, formerly leading to
a back lane and Finkle Street.
[DP234513, Alun Bull ©
Historic England Archive]

Inside back cover: Newgate Street
remains the main shopping street of
the town and at times it is brimming
with shoppers. [DP290681, Alun Bull
© Historic England Archive]

Published by Liverpool University Press on behalf of
Historic England, The Engine House, Fire Fly Avenue, Swindon SN2 2EH
www.HistoricEngland.org.uk

Historic England is a Government service championing England's heritage and giving expert,
constructive advice.

© Historic England 2023

The views expressed in this book are those of the authors and not necessarily those of Historic England.

Images (except as otherwise shown) © Historic England; Figures 12 and 52 are reproduced by permission of
Historic England Archive; Figures 14 and 23 and Chapter 2 facing page are © Historic England Archive
Aerofilms Collection; historic Ordnance Survey mapping used in figure facing pages for Chapters 4, 5 and 6 and
Figures 5 and 28 are © and database right Crown Copyright and Landmark Information Group Ltd (All rights
reserved 2023). Licence Numbers 000394 and TP0024; Map 1 on the inside cover and Map 2 on p. 106 are
based on Ordnance Survey data © Crown Copyright and database right 2023, Ordnance Survey Licence
Number 100024900.

First published 2023

ISBN 978-1-80207-838-1

British Library Cataloguing in Publication data
A CIP catalogue record for this book is available from the British Library.

For more information about images from the Archive, contact Archives Services Team, Historic England, The
Engine House, Fire Fly Avenue, Swindon SN2 2EH; telephone (01793) 414600.

Typeset in Georgia Pro Light 9.25/13pt

Page layout by Carnegie Book Production.
Printed and bound in the UK by Gomer Press.

Contents

Acknowledgements

Many colleagues at Historic England contributed towards this book. Fieldwork and research in preparation for this, and for the preceding historic area assessment, were undertaken by Clare Howard, Jayne Rimmer, Rebecca Pullen, Marcus Jecock, Sally Evans and Hilary Gould. The book is much the richer for its photography, undertaken by Alun Bull and James O Davies on the ground, and by Emma Trevarthen from the air; additional images were commissioned from Anna Bridson. Graphics support was provided by Sharon Soutar. We are very grateful to Lucy Jessop, David Went and Rebecca Pullen for their review of the manuscript and constructive feedback. The book was brought to publication by Alison Welsby at Liverpool University Press, and Sarah Davison and Lucy Frontani at Carnegie Book Production.

Local historians and authors Tom Hutchinson, Barbara Laurie and Robert McManners generously shared their knowledge, expertise and material, read drafts of the manuscript and offered many useful comments. We are indebted to them for this.

Staff at the Historic England Archive, Durham Record Office, Durham University, The Auckland Project and The College of Arms have been helpful and informative in assisting us to acquire key historical documents and images to inform and illustrate our research. A new reconstruction drawing of the railway area, skilfully prepared by Allan T. Adams, captures how the busy industrial heart of the town may once have looked.

Historic England would like to thank Durham County Council, and in particular Annalisa Ward and Anne Allen, Bishop Auckland Heritage Action Zone project managers, and Bryan Harris, conservation officer, for their invaluable assistance throughout the project. We also wish to extend our thanks to the Bishop Auckland Civic Society, chaired by Robert McManners; The Auckland Project, especially John Castling; the University of Durham, in particular Chris Gerrard; the Bishop Auckland Golf Club; and numerous other local businesses and residents who allowed us to visit their properties as part of our research.

Foreword from the Chair of Bishop Auckland Civic Society

When I was a boy, Bishop Auckland was always a grand day out; a shopping bonanza for my mother, an endless adventure playground for me, my two brothers and our dad in the Bishop's park. We learned much about the mighty Prince Bishops and the history of the County Palatine, of the stories of slain boars and of the preparations for bloody battles. Not surprising then, when, after qualifying, 'Bishop' became my adopted home of some 50 years.

Bishop Auckland is undoubtedly a place to be proud of. Throughout its history it has repeatedly risen from its lean times to prosper again as the authors of this book so succinctly inform us. In a text rich with fact, and in an easy-to-navigate chronological narrative, we are taken on a two-millennia adventure – because this town's history IS the stuff of ripping yarns.

Piecing together the town's history is not easy. Much archaeology has been lost during its many reconfigurations and Bishop Auckland, County Durham's largest town, was deprived of its place in Robert Surtees' definitive four-volume *History of the County Palatine of Durham* because of the writer's untimely death.

This book's authors have risen to the challenge of reconstructing that fragmented history and bring us bang up to date, acknowledging the civic pride of a community that rescued major buildings in their town from unnecessary destruction through the town's Civic Society, which also successfully opposed the Church Commissioners about the proposed sale of the renowned series of Zurbarán paintings – 'Jacob and his Twelve Sons'. This was a campaign which drew national attention and persuaded the philanthropist Jonathan Ruffer not only to buy the paintings, donating them to Bishop Auckland, but to invest vast sums of his private money into the town – at one of Bishop's very lean times.

The concept of regeneration through history, heritage and the arts comes through loud and clear in the conclusion of this little gem of a book, which emphasises the significance and appeal of the vernacular art of the coalminers as being at least equal to our audience as that of the classical art of antiquity.

Dr Robert McManners OBE, DL
Chair, Bishop Auckland HAZ; Chair, Bishop Auckland Civic Society

Foreword from Historic England and Durham County Council

Bishop Auckland is embarking upon its next chapter as an exciting international visitor destination. Its impressive historic buildings and open spaces tell the fascinating story of an attractive and influential market town shaped by the power of the bishops of Durham and coloured by the fluctuating fortunes of commerce and industry. From the magnificent Auckland Castle to the engineering workshops of Lingford and Gardiner, this legacy provides a strong foundation on which to build a brighter and more sustainable future for the town.

Making the past part of the future lay at the heart of our Heritage Action Zone, a successful partnership forged between Durham County Council and Historic England, complementing the major private and public investment being undertaken in the town centre, including the restoration of Auckland Castle. The HAZ involved a range of projects designed to revitalise the historic market town and to help regenerate it as a vibrant place for local people, businesses and visitors. The programme was underpinned by meticulous research to understand Bishop Auckland's development and the significance of its archaeological and architectural legacy. This knowledge and understanding will help ensure that its character and special qualities are conserved and enhanced, while allowing for sensitive management and new investment amid all the pressures for change.

This colourful and informative book offers an opportunity to explore and celebrate Bishop Auckland's wonderful history and heritage. We invite you to discover some of the stories this delightful place has to offer.

Sir Laurie Magnus CBE
Chairman of Historic England

Councillor Elizabeth Scott
Cabinet Portfolio Holder for Economy and Partnerships
Durham County Council

Newgate Street is the main shopping street in Bishop Auckland and stretches almost a mile from the Market Place to the railway station.
[DP290652, Alun Bull © Historic England Archive]

1

Introduction

Set in a landscape of gently undulating valleys and hills, the historic market town of Bishop Auckland holds a commanding position on a natural plateau high above a wide, distinctive meander in the River Wear, its tributary the Gaunless snaking along the town's eastern edge. From the north, the towers, spires and arches of some of Bishop Auckland's key historic landmarks enliven the tree-filled scene, while within the town lies a rich collection of buildings from many centuries and an archaeological legacy spanning two millennia (Fig. 1).

The Bishop Auckland of today was born of a small two-row village to which a busy market was added before transforming into a thriving industrial town, its prospects shaped and bolstered by its strategic location and the power of its long and close association with the bishops of Durham. This has forged an attractive town whose great strength of character is expressed by its people and architecture alike.

Beyond the small but splendid castle, the buildings seen in the town today were mostly constructed in the 18th and 19th centuries. They tell the story of an increasingly important centre of trade, industry, civic pride and culture. By the late 19th century, Bishop Auckland was booming, its economy driven by the mining industry and railways; by 1881 the town's population of about 12,000 was six times that recorded only 60 years before. But like many parts of the north-east of England, it was affected by the demise of coal mining and engineering from the mid-20th century onwards. With the 21st-century impact of out-of-town and online shopping, the town centre began to see vacant buildings in a deteriorating condition. The town's conservation area was added to the national Heritage at Risk Register in 2011.

As a response to this and the enthusiasm of local people for their town, Bishop Auckland received intensive support from Historic England's Heritage Action Zone (HAZ) initiative. This programme set out to transform the fortunes of the town's historic environment, stimulating economic growth to bring neglected buildings back into use, improve the townscape, and kickstart regeneration and renewal. The Bishop Auckland HAZ ran for five years from April 2018, a partnership between Historic England, Durham County Council, the Brighter Bishop Auckland Regeneration Partnership and local people, brought together through an advisory group. By focusing on the main historic town streets – Market Place, Newgate Street and Fore Bondgate – the HAZ complemented the major ongoing programme of investment at and around the

This aerial photograph, taken from the south-east in 2018, shows Auckland Castle and the historic market place perched on the high plateau above the rivers. [34095_026, Emma Trevarthen © Historic England Archive]

1

Figure 1
The colourful mix of stone and brick buildings with red
and grey rooftops against the green rolling hills of
Weardale makes Bishop Auckland a particularly
attractive market town.
[DP234702, Alun Bull © Historic England Archive]

castle by The Auckland Project (TAP), whose vision is to rejuvenate the town as an international visitor destination. Today, Bishop Auckland seems set to enter a new and vibrant chapter, one where unlocking the exciting potential of historic streets and buildings is creating a spirited cultural and commercial prospect for local people and visitors.

This book brings together research into the town's archaeology, history and architecture that was carried out to guide the HAZ. Although the medieval and post-medieval history of Auckland Castle and parkland is fairly well known, this is not the case for the town. Its first comprehensive history was written by Matthew Richley in his 1872 publication, *The History and Characteristics of Bishop Auckland*, and while it still provides a thorough historical account of the town, it is very much a product of its time. It is only in more recent years that the town has been researched by local historians, notably Tom Hutchinson and Barbara Laurie. These authors explore its social and economic development – particularly during the 19th and 20th centuries – and both have amassed and published a tremendous collection of postcards and photographs. Their work sheds light on the built environment, revealing buildings and streets that have long been demolished, or changes to those which have stood the test of time.

Historic England's research builds on this work, focusing on the development of the town centre to help understand what makes its built heritage so special, in order to inspire and inform sound protection for the future. A team of architectural, archaeological and aerial survey investigators carried out a historic area assessment of the town's core and Auckland Castle Park, which was published in the Historic England Research Report Series in 2021, together with a further report concentrating on the town's road, rail and parkland bridges. Specific buildings in the HAZ were investigated, including the former Central Stores of the Bishop Auckland Co-operative Society (no. 80 Newgate Street, until recently Beales department store); the former McIntyre's shoe shop at no. 25 Newgate Street, with its beautiful Art Nouveau-inspired shopfront; and the handsome but forlorn former Bishop Auckland Mechanics Institute at no. 27 Victoria Avenue. All of these reports are publicly available online.[1]

At the time of writing, the urban core of Bishop Auckland has seen very limited archaeological investigation and still hides many of the secrets of its history and development, particularly prior to the 18th century. However, a current Bishop Big Dig initiative – exploring private gardens across the town through small-scale excavation – is starting to fill some of these gaps. As the current period of research, investment and rejuvenation of the town, castle and park unfolds, the pace of change is high and new information is continually coming to light. This book is in no sense a definitive work on the history, archaeology and architecture of Bishop Auckland, but it aims to highlight their most significant aspects and to offer insights into the rich built heritage and half-hidden stories that surround those who visit, live and work in this important place today.

2   Early archaeology

Settlement before 1700

Evidence for prehistoric activity within Bishop Auckland is limited, as much of the archaeology has either been lost or buried due to clearance and occupation from the medieval period onwards. However, a small number of prehistoric artefacts, including a double-edged flint blade, have been discovered within the area of Auckland Castle and parkland.[2] While these artefacts are not definitive evidence of early occupation, the elongated plateau on which the present-day castle sits could well have been exploited as an obvious strategic position for a fort or settlement.

Situated approximately 0.9 miles (1.5km) to the north of modern Bishop Auckland are the extensive remains of the Roman fort and associated settlement (*vicus*) of Binchester (*Vinovia* or *Vinovium*), established in AD 69–75 and occupied until at least the 5th century. The site has been the focus of much research and investigation which is ongoing, and today the impressive structures of two excavated bath houses provide the focus for a visitor centre and education facilities. The proximity to Binchester, along with the meeting point of Roman roads just outside the town and the high vantage point afforded from the plateau, may have drawn associated human activity to within the footprint of the modern town. The main route of Newgate Street is thought to overlie part of the major Roman road of Dere Street that ran from York to Corbridge (via Binchester) and then on to the fort at Cramond (Edinburgh) with its links to the Antonine Wall. In 1872, Matthew Richley wrote that the remains of a well-preserved road surface, believed to be Dere Street, were discovered during the laying of new sewers at Newgate End (now Newgate Street) and Fenkle (later Finkle) Street. The course of this suspected Roman route disappears as Newgate Street enters the market place and it is difficult to determine which onward path it would have taken to reach Binchester. A direct route would have roughly followed the line of the present Wear Chare, but if it continued on the same trajectory, this would have required two crossings over the loop of the River Wear, a rather costly and perhaps unnecessary undertaking. Alternatively, the road may have turned east and then north, following the outer bank of the river, or perhaps cut through the area now occupied by Auckland Castle Park. Certainly, a cremation urn was discovered in the vicinity of Bishop Trevor's parkland bridge across the River Gaunless when it was built in 1757 and further

An aerial photograph taken in 1947 showing the town with its tightly packed long tenement plots before the road improvements of the later 20th century. [EAW005552 © Historic England Archive]

burials were found in this area during the laying of sewers in 1938. Roman burials were often placed outside settlements and alongside key routeways.[3]

Early medieval evidence

The name Bishop Auckland, first used in the 14th century, reflected the status of the settlement as one of the main residences of the bishops of Durham. Prior to this, it was known as North Auckland and was first referenced as such in a charter dating between 995 and 1006 that granted land to the community of St Cuthbert (who resided at Durham). The charter also names neighbouring settlements, including Binchester, Escomb and also *Weardseatle*, a pre-Norman term meaning guarded seat. It is interesting to conjecture that *Weardseatle* may have stood on the promontory that was to become the site of Auckland Castle. Some of the local names, or elements thereof, still used today may have pre-Anglo Saxon or Scandinavian origins, including Auckland, Wear and Gaunless. North Auckland was not the pre-Norman parochial centre, however. This lay, and continues to lie, at St Andrew's, with its deanery located in South Church, 1.1 miles (1.8km) to the south of the castle (*see* Chapter 4 facing page). This church was largely rebuilt in the 13th century but remnants of an 8th- or 9th-century cross shaft have been reused within the tower.

The arrival of the bishops

The County Palatine of Durham, effectively an earldom, was established in 1075 and gave the bishops of Durham great secular and civic authority. The bishops continued to gain land and power, and in 1109 part of the Forest of Weardale, which included Auckland Castle Park, was given by Henry I to Bishop Ranulf Flambard. Auckland Castle Park became one of the oldest and largest of the estates held by the bishops of Durham. It is mentioned in *Boldon Book* (or *Boldon Buke*), compiled in 1183, along with a more detailed account of the settlement at North Auckland which lists some of the landowners and tenants as well as tenures, descent of properties and services rendered to the bishop.[4] Some historians argue that it was around this date that the settlement was first formally laid out, with the establishment of a large market place and rows of long narrow plots along its north and south sides (*see* p. 4 and p. 12). The survey lists 22 villeins (feudal tenant farmers, later known as bondagers or bondsmen), each holding one bovate or oxgang (about 20 or 32 acres depending on the type of measuring tool used) who provided grain and labour to support the demesne (the lord's home farm) located at Auckland Castle.

The earliest part of the present Auckland Castle is believed to be the hall built by Bishop du Puiset and transformed into the Chapel of St Peter in the 17th century. The hall was adapted and extended into the grand palace and hunting lodge for Bishop Bek (in office 1284–1310/1), known as Auckland Manor or Hall until about 1500. The stone manor house comprised a new great hall (now the throne room), possibly a four-storey block of private apartments and a two-storey chapel all enclosed within stone walls. The chapel was demolished in the 17th century, but excavations undertaken between 2020 and 2022 have revealed the remains of a substantial, very grand and sumptuous two-storey building which would have rivalled some of the finest churches in the country at the time (Fig. 2).

By 1381, when a survey was commissioned by Bishop Hatfield (known as the Hatfield Survey), the settlement of North Auckland had grown to accommodate 17 cottagers (peasants with little or no land), 20 tenants holding demesne lands (land on the lord's farm) of 134 acres and 22 tenants holding demesne lands of 79 acres.[5] Some of the tenants are named, including Johannes Pollard, who owned various detached parcels of land throughout the town. Despite the family seemingly dying out within the area in the 16th century, these parcels remained a separate township until 1894 when they were amalgamated with the civil parish of Bishop Auckland. A survey compiled in 1647 suggests that the land parcels had been given to the Pollard family as payment for killing a wild boar that caused havoc in the park and surrounding area.[6] The family were certainly of higher status than most of their neighbours and, according to Richley, are believed to have held a large manor house located on the south side of the market place (demolished in about 1810 and replaced by the Barrington School). These detached 'Pollards Lands' are shown scattered across the town on the 1857 Ordnance Survey town plan (*see* Fig. 5).

The bishops continued to make various additions and improvements during the medieval period, improving the accommodation and amenities at Auckland

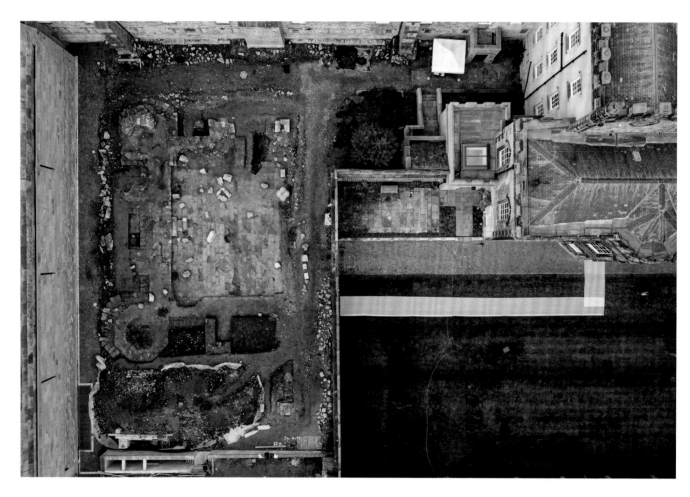

Castle, and within the surrounding parkland. The most notable of these was the addition of an ecclesiastical college within the castle precinct in the mid-15th century, relocated from the deanery at St Andrew's in South Church. The quadrangular college is located on the north side of the modern castle approach with a wide archway leading into it on its south side (Fig. 3).[7] The building has been modified to accommodate smaller cottages, but blocked mullioned windows and a doorway attest to its date and former function. The medieval

Figure 2
A vertical view of the impressive west end of Bek's chapel during excavation in 2022. The white sheet is laid out to indicate the line of the south wall of the chapel.
[© Durham University/Alexander Jansen]

park was very much a productive landscape. It held deer, wild white cattle, draught oxen and sheep, and included fishponds, meadow for fodder and grazing, a fulling mill and pits for mineral extraction. While the area within the modern park boundary has always been a core element, documentary evidence and clues in the landscape show that the full extent of the park has expanded and contracted several times since its establishment. Indeed, recent mapping from aerial sources identified the curving arc of a ditch running east and north-east of the modern park, which probably represents a parkland boundary (perhaps a park pale) from one of these earlier phases (Fig. 4).

Figure 3
The 15th-century college at Auckland Castle, transformed into cottages and outbuildings in the 19th century and now a mixture of offices, outbuildings and domestic properties.
[DP290671, Alun Bull © Historic England Archive]

Bank or mound

Ditch or drain

Quarry

Ridge and furrow

Slope or scarp

0   100   200m

Figure 4
Archaeological features within the parkland were mapped from aerial survey and ground-based field observations in 2019 by Historic England.
[Sharon Soutar © Historic England]

1 – Auckland Castle
2 – deer shelter
3 – main drive
4 – Bishop Trevor's bridge
5 – ice house
6 – site of Middle Lodge
7 – Bishop's Bridge (over railway)
8 – Park Head
9 – well head
10 – possible park pale
11 – tree enclosure ring
12 – possible carriage drive

The medieval market place

Auckland Castle has always been somewhat detached from the rest of the town, separated from the historic centre by a high wall and prominent gatehouse. It sits at the broad end of the quadrilateral market place, which is formed by the convergence of Wear Chare, Castle Chare and Bondgate (now North Bondgate, Fore Bondgate and High Bondgate). The main road from Durham entered the town from the east along Durham Chare via a river crossing in the location of the current Gaunless Bridge, before climbing up the hill to meet Newgate Street. The word 'chare' is a term often used in north-east England to describe a narrow street, lane or alley; its medieval origins suggest that the routes may have been established (or at least reaffirmed) at or around the same time as the market place and the bishop's palace in the 12th century.[8]

The market place seems to have been tacked on to the east end of an existing village that comprised two rows of properties fronting onto a wide village green. Vestiges of long plots, each reminiscent of a toft (house with a small garden) fronting the green with a long croft (for growing crops and grazing animals) behind, can be seen on the 1857 Ordnance Survey map along the north side of North Bondgate and the south side of the market place stretching along the steep slopes towards The Batts (Fig. 5). Similar medieval plots were probably once located along the south side of High Bondgate and Fore Bondgate, although they have been much altered. These plots were most likely occupied by the villeins (bondsmen, tenants dependent upon and in the service of the bishop), hence the name 'Bondgate'.

As the settlement grew, the tofts and crofts – especially in the economically more valuable area of the later market place – were probably subdivided into narrower plots known as burgages in order to maximise income from burghers or burgesses (traders or privileged inhabitants) whose properties did not need the width of the entire street frontage of the earlier tofts (assuming the village ever extended this far east). The narrower, longer plots along the north and south side of the market place take this form. Vaulted undercrofts have been identified underneath no. 7 on the south side of the market place (potentially part of Pollard's Hall) and at no. 38 (former Queen's Head) on the north side, which may date back to the medieval period.

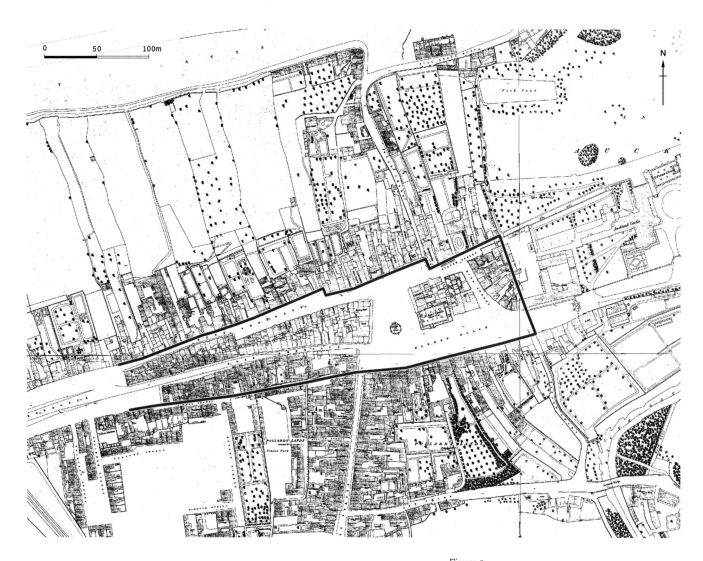

Medieval undercrofts had a wide range of uses and could be leased separately from the buildings above them.

The first reference to a chapel of ease within the market place, presumably on the site of the present Church of St Anne (built in 1846–8), appears in a

Figure 5
Extract from the Ordnance Survey 1:500 Town Plan published in 1857 (surveyed 1856), with overlay depicting the suggested extent of the medieval market place.

document dated 1391 referring to a grant of land for the chapel's extension. The medieval chapel was extended in 1424 and 1452, but had fallen into ruin by 1638. It stood within or beside a central green known as St Anne's Green.[9] Newgate Street formed the main route into the market place from the south during the medieval period and was similarly lined on its east and west sides with tenement plots between its north end and Durham Chare. These plots, however, were not as long as those found elsewhere within the market place, perhaps owing in part to their curtailment by north–south plots along the south sides of the market place and Fore Bondgate. This suggests that they are a later extension of the medieval settlement.

Fore Bondgate provided an east–west route through the centre of the market place. It may initially have been lined with temporary stalls which were then gradually replaced by more permanent structures. The practice of encroachment onto a former open market area took place elsewhere in other towns in England after about 1300. An earthenware jug dating from the 13th or 14th century was discovered at the corner of Fore Bondgate and Newgate Street in 1907 when a well at the Talbot Inn was being cleared.[10] The present buildings along Fore Bondgate, however, date from the 18th and 19th centuries, although it is possible that earlier fabric remains hidden. The Bay Horse public house is certainly thought to have replaced a 15th- or early 16th-century building when it was rebuilt in the early 20th century; remnants of an earlier stone building can be seen within the side elevation of the present building.

16th-century Bishop Auckland

In his *Itinerary of England and Wales* compiled between 1535 and 1543, John Leland describes Bishop Auckland as 'of no estimation', with the exception of a pretty corn market.[11] He goes on to describe the topography and castle in great detail, including the impressive medieval hall (inaccurately ascribed to Bishop Bek) with black marble pillars speckled with white. The earliest maps to depict Bishop Auckland are the county maps drawn by John Rudd (published in 1569) and Christopher Saxton's map of 1576 (Fig. 6). The Saxton map is the more accurate of the two and shows two crossings: one over the River Wear, presumably in the location of Newton

Figure 6
Extract from Saxton's 1576 County Map of Durham
centred on Bishop Auckland.
[DRO D/CL 23/2 Reproduced by permission of Durham
County Record Office]

Cap Bridge, and the second over the Gaunless, roughly in the location of the present Gaunless Bridge. Newton Cap Bridge was probably built in the 16th or 17th century to replace a bridge built in the 14th century by Bishop Skirlaw. The present Gaunless Bridge is 18th century with a 19th-century addition. Saxton uses an image of a large fortified building – no doubt the bishops' palace – to depict the town, rather than a house or a church as is used in the representation of most settlements.

It is possible that 16th-century buildings survive as hidden fabric behind later frontages, although many have been entirely replaced. One, with a low elevation, steep sloping roof and mullioned windows, previously stood on the site of the former Queen's Head public house (no. 38 Market Place); it was replaced by the present building in about 1898.[12] A building of similar size and proportions is located at no. 69 Newgate Street (Fig. 7). Furthermore, a building described by Richley in 1872 as 'a very old Elizabethan building, with projecting windows like buttresses with stone mullions, which was the principal inn of the town' once also stood along Newgate Street at the point where Tenters Street was later cut through. The Chapter House (nos 35 and

Figure 7
No. 69 Newgate Street, possibly a survivor of the 16th century.
[DP290662, Alun Bull © Historic England Archive]

37 High Bondgate) is also thought to be one of the oldest buildings surviving within the town, built of stone rubble and with a steeply pitched roof.

Change and investment in the 17th century

Many of the open fields surrounding Bishop Auckland were enclosed during the first half of the 17th century. At about this time there was a great deal of investment in Auckland Castle and the parkland, and the park was vastly increased in size. Steady economic growth in the town was interrupted by the English Civil Wars (1642–51) and Oliver Cromwell's Protectorate (1651–9), which saw much of the power and authority held by the archbishops and bishops suppressed, and their lands and possessions confiscated and placed under centralised control. In response to this, a Parliamentary Survey of the bishop's estates in the County Palatine, including the Manor of Auckland and the

'Ruines of the Castle or Pallace of Bishop Auckland' was compiled in 1646–7.[13] The survey describes Bishop Auckland as a busy market centre with a weekly market held on Thursdays, a Borough Court held once a fortnight and fairs held twice a year. Tolls were paid to the bishop via a toll booth within the market place, probably at the Market Cross. Some of the surrounding fields were used for arable farming and there were two corn mills on the Gaunless (Burne Mill) and the Wear (West Mill), as well as a fulling mill (in disrepair), a new dye house and pits for the extraction of lime. The King's Highway (presumably the main road from Durham) and Gib Chare (now Durham Chare) are mentioned, but individual landholdings are listed only by name of the landowner or tenant and so their locations are difficult to identify within the town today. Auckland Castle is described in some detail as a stately manor house comprising two chapels, stables, brewhouse, bakehouse and other offices, and with a gatehouse and stone walls enclosing the perimeter. Auckland Castle Park was enclosed by drystone walls and timber pales and was modestly stocked with rabbit, fallow deer and wild cattle. This area was separate from the wider park, which was largely open meadow.

Auckland Manor, including Auckland Castle and Park, was purchased by the parliamentarian military leader Sir Arthur Hesilrige [Haselrig] in 1648, following his rise to the position of governor of Newcastle in the preceding year. Hesilrige made vast alterations to the castle, including the demolition of Bishop Bek's two-storey medieval chapel before he embarked on the construction of a lavish Italian-style mansion. The new house was never completed because Hesilrige was imprisoned in the Tower of London upon the restoration of the monarchy in 1660. The bishopric was re-established under Bishop John Cosin (in office 1660–72), who embarked upon an ambitious programme to restore the dilapidated palace buildings and parkland. This included the transformation of du Puiset's medieval hall into the episcopal Chapel of St Peter and the construction of a new dining hall, episcopal library and walls around the inner courtyards.[14] He also improved the park, including the renewal of the fishponds, and enclosed the garden on the south side of the castle (completed by 1728).

A pen-and-ink drawing created in 1666 by Gregory King, showing the prospect of the town and castle from the east, is perhaps the earliest detailed depiction of Bishop Auckland. This drawing demonstrates that the town had expanded beyond its medieval core by the middle of the 17th century (Fig. 8).[15]

The main thoroughfare of Bondgate (separated into two parallel streets) and Newgate are clearly depicted and labelled, as well as the main route from Durham along Durham Chare climbing up the hill towards Newgate Street. The narrower route of Castle Chare can be seen squeezed between the long tenement plots that slope down the south side of the plateau from the market place. There are clusters of buildings within the market place and along the main routes, although it is difficult to identify them individually. The castle stretches out to the east of the market place and is surrounded by imposing stone walls. The extent to which the medieval buildings remain standing suggest that Hesilrige's destruction of the palace may not have been as extensive as Cosin and his contemporaries had suggested (Fig. 9).

Figure 8
Gregory King's prospect of the castle, chapel and town of Bishop Auckland, 1666.
[College of Arms MS C. 41, Durham Church Notes, fol. 10b. Reproduced by permission of the Kings, Heralds and Pursuivants of Arms]

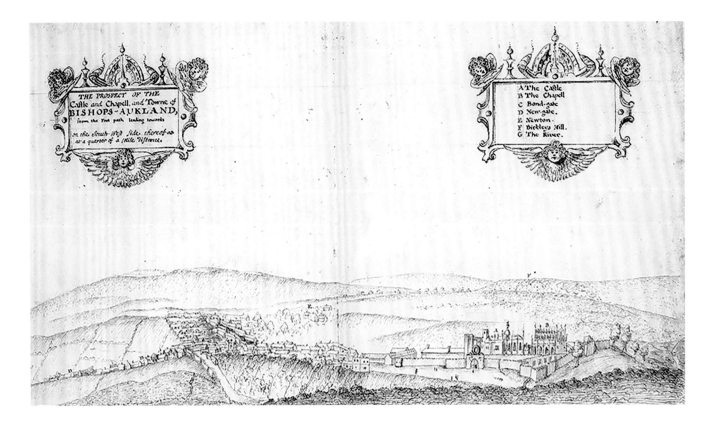

Surviving 17th-century buildings within the town are limited. They are largely concentrated on the eastern side of the market place (nos 22, 23, 24 and 25), close to and perhaps formerly associated with the castle. These tall and attractive houses, built on the road previously known as King Street, mostly have two or three storeys with basements and attics. They are constructed of stone

Figure 9
A painting of Auckland Castle from the south-east by an unknown artist, in about 1680, showing the extent of the surviving medieval buildings following Cosin's improvements.
[CC.2012.39 Courtesy of The Auckland Project and The Church Commissioners]

which is now rendered, with steeply pitched roofs, stone coping and kneelers, similar to those depicted in a painting of the castle and town of about 1700, showing the cluster of buildings in the market place (Fig. 10). Other good examples of 17th-century buildings include no. 30 Market Place, also known as the Sportsman (previously known as the Merry Monk) public house, which has a range fronting Market Place with similar late 17th-century features.

The survival of the medieval layout of the town – particularly the convergence of the main routeways within the market place, vestiges of early village tenement plots and the juxtaposition of the town with the bishops' manor, which have been preserved for over 800 years – is remarkable and

Figure 10
A somewhat romanticised painting of Auckland Castle from the south-east by an unknown artist, dated about 1700. The castle is given an exaggerated elevated position with dramatic steep slopes on its south side falling to the River Gaunless below; the town extends to the west and the main Durham Road along Durham Chare is clearly shown.
[CC.2012.40 Courtesy of The Auckland Project and The Church Commissioners]

Figure 11
Complex phasing visible in the west elevation of nos 6
and 7 North Bondgate (part of nos 65–66 Fore
Bondgate) shows that earlier buildings have often been
incorporated into later ones, particularly with regard to
party walls.
[DP393031, Anna Bridson © Historic England Archive]

remains easily readable today. Although much of the documented general history of Bishop Auckland before 1700 is well established, the archaeological evidence is yet to be uncovered. This is partly because the 18th- and 19th-century buildings may mask earlier hidden fabric and buried remains and partly due to redevelopment taking place before archaeological investigation and recording became a requirement under national planning policy in 1990 (PPG16), particularly where major schemes such as the Newgate Shopping Centre were concerned (Fig. 11). This gap in knowledge is beginning to be addressed with a renewed research interest in the area by Durham University, The Auckland Project and others.

Blacket Esq.

Hunwick

High Birtley

Picksly Hill

Hermitsheugh

Farnly

Whins

Far Birtley

Old Park

Old Park Lodge

Bishop Close

T. Wharton Esq.

M

22

less

Near Birtley

Binchester

Wren Esq.

Lodge

Dinovium

Turnpike

121

Westerton

Mi St.

Bacon Esq.

Plass

Newton Cap.

Head

The Bishops

Palace and Park

Cundon

BISHOP AUCKLAND

19

20

Low Etherly

Black Boy

Cundon Grange

therly oor

Hen Knowle

18

Brakes

St Andrew Auckland

Ho. Robt. Esq.

Wood uses

Ox Close

G.Watling

Low Deanery

High Deanery

Close Hoise

3

Bishop Auckland in the 18th century

In the 18th century Bishop Auckland was an up-and-coming market town, with much to offer visitors and residents alike. Thomas Cox described it in his *Magna Britannia* (published in 1738) as 'one of the best in the County' of Durham, 'pleasantly seated upon the Side of an Hill, in a very good Air' and with 'handsome' houses. The map of the County Palatine of Durham by Captain Armstrong and Thomas Jeffreys (printed in 1791) shows the extent of the town and the Bishops Palace and Park (*see* facing page). The town itself was still mainly focused on the medieval market place and Bondgate, with further development along Durham Chare, the north end of Kingsway and Newgate Street.

Improvements to the main routes into and through the town greatly benefited the local economy. In 1747, the Bowes and Sunderland Bridge Turnpike Trust was formed by an Act of Parliament to manage the toll road for horse-drawn vehicles from Bowes to Sunderland Bridge in Durham, via Barnard Castle, Staindrop and Bishop Auckland.[16] Gaunless Bridge, which carried the toll road, was rebuilt in 1762 as part of these improvements. The earliest part of Jock's Bridge, which carried the road north to Binchester across the mouth of the River Gaunless, also dates to the 18th century (it was partially rebuilt in 1819). Key upgrades such as these provided the town and the castle with a safe and reliable transport network, encouraging new trade as well as improving the regular journeys made by the bishops travelling to and from Durham.

During the course of the 18th century the bishops, especially Bishop Richard Trevor (in office 1752–71), invested heavily in the castle and the parkland, and it continued to be their favoured residence, with Durham remaining the ceremonial centre of the bishop's authority until 1832.

Auckland Castle and parkland

The first major change to Auckland Castle Park during this period of investment and modification was the enhancement of the expansive walled gardens, first shown on the painting of about 1700 (*see* Fig. 10) and completed by 1728. Facing south to capture the sun and situated in a conspicuous position on the slopes beneath the castle complex, the garden was one of the largest of its kind

Detail of Bishop Auckland from Armstrong and Jeffreys' 1768 map of the County Palatine of Durham, printed 1791.
[DRO D/LO/P239 Reproduced by permission of Durham County Record Office]

in northern England at the time. Samuel and Nathaniel Buck's engraving of the palace shows part of the garden, which appears to be laid out in a regimented scheme, perhaps as a carefully managed orchard (Fig. 12). In 1757, Bishop Trevor added hothouses and heated walls; the remains of some flues and other features associated with these structures are still present in the upper, northern parts of the garden. The hothouses were probably used for growing exotic fruits such as peaches or pineapples, a symbol of a high-status household.

In 1760 a new gatehouse (also known as the Clock Tower) was built at the east end of the market place. This impressive structure was designed by the architect Sir Thomas Robinson (1702/3–77) in a Gothick Revival style and houses a 12th-century bell reused from elsewhere in the castle (Fig. 13). Earlier gatehouses (since removed) were positioned closer to the main range of

Figure 12
Samuel and Nathaniel Buck, engraving of 'The south-east view of Bishop Auckland Palace…,' dated 1728. The walled garden is only partly shown on the steep slope to the river on the left-hand side of the drawing.
[PLB/N070723 © Historic England Archive]

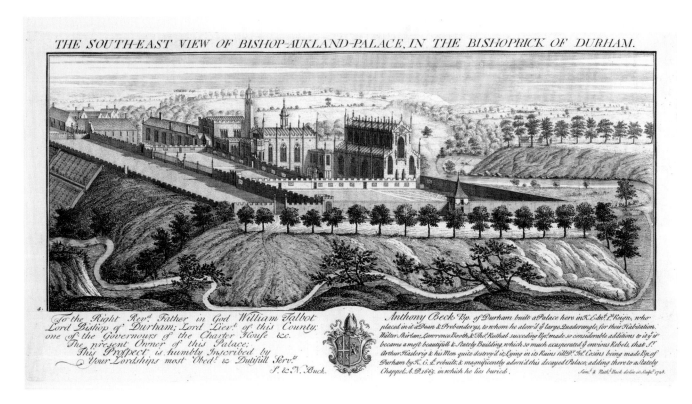

THE SOUTH-EAST VIEW OF BISHOP-AUKLAND-PALACE, IN THE BISHOPRICK OF DURHAM.

Auckland Castle, but this new one was in a much more prominent location nearer to the market place, reaffirming the boundary between the castle and the town. Slotted in between existing buildings to the north and south of the castle approach, it also allowed greater control of access to the castle and parkland beyond. At the same time, the 17th-century Castle Lodge was purchased by Bishop Trevor and repurposed as a porter's lodge. The erection of a gatehouse in this location was a renewed statement of the wealth and power of the bishops, creating a grand ceremonial entrance to herald the arrival of residents and guests.

Figure 13
The gatehouse to Auckland Castle and buildings lining the approach from Market Place, viewed from the west. Castle Lodge is visible in the background on the right and the former College with its recently reinstated archway is seen on the left.
[DP290659, Alun Bull © Historic England Archive]

Major building and repair works were carried out at Auckland Castle during the second half of the 18th century, providing new spaces for entertaining and private rooms for residents and guests, and upgrading existing facilities (Fig. 14). An imposing two-storey block with a large, eye-catching canted bay window was built on the south side of the complex to house Bishop Trevor's private apartments. This accompanied a further suite of rooms built on the north side, to the west of the chapel. The projecting south porch at the west end of the chapel was also heightened to provide further private apartments. In addition to this, windows were replaced with sashes set within a mixture of square- and ogee-headed surrounds, and interiors modernised (particularly the Long Dining Room and King Charles Bedroom which were lavishly refurbished), making them much more comfortable and welcoming. At the end of the 18th century, an impressive crenellated screen wall with a grand entrance gate was erected along the length of the gardens in front of the castle (Fig. 15). It was designed by James Wyatt (1746–1813) around 1795–7 in a Gothick Revival style; its series of pointed arches frame views of the castle and chapel.

Bishop Trevor also placed his mark on the parkland. He was greatly influenced by the writer and landscape gardener Joseph Spence (1699–1768),

who in 1754 advised him on how the parkland could be enhanced to improve its scenic qualities. Among his written notes, Spence observed that 'The Gaunless itself looks narrow … and is too much deserted of water in all dry times' and he questioned how 'far it might be raised, and widened, by 2 or 3 Dams or Rocky Stoppages at proper intervals'.[17] The manipulation of the river's flow to create a series of cascades, ornamental riffles and still sections (in part to create a reflective, mirrored surface), along with the creation of new paths and rides through the park, tree-planting designs and other enhancements, were largely a result of Spence's ideas.

Figure 16
'A plan of the park and demesnes at Auckland Castle …
taken in 1772 by Jeremiah Dixon'.
[Courtesy of The Auckland Project and The Church
Commissioners]

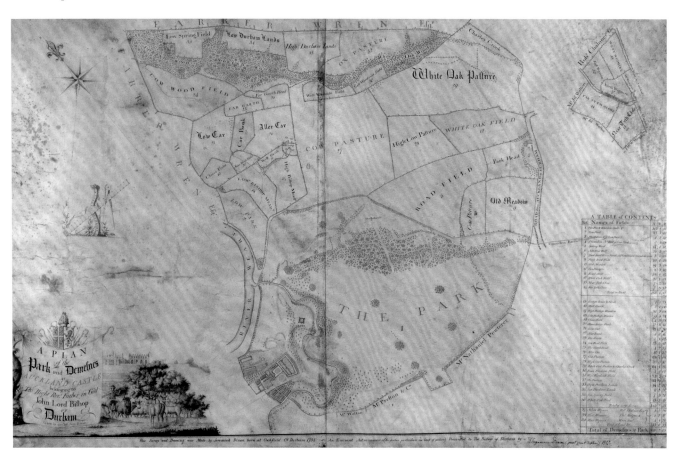

Figure 17
The deer shelter in Auckland Castle Park within its
landscape context, viewed from the north-east.
[DP290656, Alun Bull © Historic England Archive]

The parkland was loosely divided into two areas: the Inner Park west of the Gaunless and closest to Auckland Castle, and the Outer Park comprising the High Park north of the Coundon Burn and the High Plain, now occupied by the golf course (Fig. 16). A large deer house with a two-storey tower, a crenellated external arcade and tall corner buttresses topped with pinnacles was built on a raised area of ground in the Inner Park in about 1760 (Fig. 17). This eye-catcher is thought to have been designed by Thomas Wright (1711–86), astronomer, architect and garden designer, who went to school in Bishop Auckland. As well as providing shelter and food for the park's deer, it also contained a prospect room in the tower for enjoying the view.

In the High Park, a series of new bridges was erected across the valleys of the River Gaunless and the Coundon Burn. The largest and finest of these is Bishop Richard Trevor's masonry arch road bridge carrying the main drive across the River Gaunless, which has a date stone inscribed with 'RD 1757' (RD stands for 'Richard Dunelm', or Richard of Durham). An ornamental well head marked by a four-sided stone pyramid on a square plinth, sometimes known as 'The Obelisk', also acts as an eye-catcher in the High Park. The end of the drive on the north-east side of the park is marked by a set of ornate stone park gates and screen walls, probably also designed by James Wyatt. This route connected Auckland Castle and parkland with the road to Durham and, in contrast to the main ceremonial entrance in the market place, provided a more private entrance into the complex.

The town

While Bishop Trevor was carrying out his ambitious plans in and around Auckland Castle, the town was undergoing a similar transformation, with new buildings replacing older structures across the market place, North Bondgate, Fore Bondgate, High Bondgate and Newgate Street. The market place was the focal point of the town, holding a weekly market on Thursdays in addition to two annual fairs for the sale of cattle, sheep, swine and horses. At the centre of the wide, open space was a covered Market Cross, standing between Fore Bondgate and the church. It took the form of a market hall with shops and a toll booth, and it was probably similar to the one at Barnard Castle (dated 1747). Due to decay, it was replaced in 1797 with a market house located in a new square tower added to the Chapel of St Anne.[18] The chapel was itself rebuilt in 1781–3, with a room for King James I Grammar School and a justice room for local magistrates on the ground floor.[19] The town's stocks were prominently positioned near to the western end of the new tower, along with the public pant (fountain), which supplied drinking water piped from Auckland Castle Park.

There were several inns in the market place, of which the King's Arms and the Talbot Inn were known to be the largest and best. The King's Arms, later the Post Chaise, still stands on the north side of the market place. The Talbot occupied a prominent position on the south corner of Market Place and Fore Bondgate until it was demolished in the late 20th century (although it had already been extensively modified resulting in the loss of its distinctive corner turret). By the early 19th century a stagecoach operated daily from the Talbot, which also served as the town's posting house and excise office.

Public assembly rooms were built on Fore Bondgate (nos 10 and 11) in the early 18th century, providing wealthy townspeople with a place to meet and enjoy a range of entertainments, including balls, concerts and card playing

(Fig. 18). This complex also had important civic functions: the magistrates' courts were held there before the police station was built in 1856 and the town council also met there before the town hall was constructed in the market place in 1861. When first built, the assembly rooms were said to have been one of the most prominent buildings in the town, boasting a lead-covered roof terrace from which guests were able to view the Auckland racecourse on the north bank of the River Wear. The Ordnance Survey map published in 1857 shows that there were also extensive landscaped gardens to the rear (later the site of the auction mart) which extended south all the way to Tenters Street, now the site of the Newgate Shopping Centre (*see* Fig. 5).

Now a rather unassuming building divided into two properties, nos 10 and 11 Fore Bondgate still retain a sense of grandeur, with prominent rusticated stone quoins emphasising the corners, a deep stone plinth at the base, and heavily rusticated stone window and doorway surrounds. The high-ceilinged first-floor rooms would have been accessed from the central doorway and their tall windows would have provided ample light. The building was already divided and occupied by two separate households by the time of the 1851 census.[20] The

Figure 18
Nos 10–11 Fore Bondgate, the 18th-century former assembly rooms, viewed from the north-west.
[DP290685, Alun Bull © Historic England Archive]

1871 census listed no. 11 as the Shepherd's Inn and, when the whole building was advertised for sale in 1875, it was described as a hotel and a private dwelling.[21]

To the rear of the building, running below Finkle Street, was an interesting feature known locally as the 'Doctor's Tunnel'. Local lore has it that a doctor who held a surgery at the Shepherd's Inn requested that his poorer patients waited in the tunnel to be seen, while the wealthier patients entered by the main entrance on Fore Bondgate. By 1901 no. 10 was occupied by ice-cream maker and merchant Giuseppe Dimambro and no. 11 had become the Ye Oakland Hotel.[22] It has remained as two properties ever since and has been much altered inside, including the insertion of an extra floor which required the first-floor windows to be reduced in height.

As the number of high-status houses shows, Market Place became an exclusive place to live. The 18th-century buildings each have an individual character, showcasing a range of materials and architectural embellishments. On the south side of Market Place there are two large red-brick houses which date to this period: no. 5 is now a public house (the Stanley Jefferson) and no. 4 was originally the vicarage of the Church of St Andrew (Fig. 19). Both buildings were built from narrow, red, handmade bricks with stone details, such as the quoins to the east side of no. 4, gable copings and moulded kneelers to the roof. They each have elaborate door surrounds and overlights. No. 5 originally extended all the way down to Durham Chare (now bisected by Kingsway) and still has an extensive range of outhouses to the rear, including what may have once been a stable. The main building has a striking two-storey bowed projection with large windows at the front, making it particularly eye-catching within the market place. It was occupied from at least the early 19th century by the Bowser family, who practiced law and had a long-standing connection with Bishop Auckland, owning large amounts of land and holding various offices within the bishopric.

The Elms, set back on the north side of Market Place, is a grand, three-storey mid-18th-century town house with a red-brick façade, ashlar quoins, and a prominent Ionic porch and doorway (Fig. 20). This building is not quite what it seems, however, as the rest is constructed of stone rubble and there are at least two main phases of construction, suggesting that The Elms is an older structure refronted and modified in the 18th century. The eastern elevation is especially complex, with several different phases of stonework suggesting multiple

Figure 19
Buildings along the south side of the market place, including no. 4 Market Place, the former vicarage of the Church of St Andrew, and no. 5, the Stanley Jefferson public house.
[DP290648, Alun Bull © Historic England Archive]

alterations and additions (Fig. 21). The building originally sat within a large plot with landscaped gardens to the front and rear. The front garden wall, matching the red brick of the front elevation of the house, survives intact with ashlar plinth, copings, central gate piers and niches. A two-storey range with a carriage entrance was also added to the west in the 18th century.

These grand examples would have stood alongside smaller housing. As the *Universal British Directory of Trade, Commerce, and Manufacture* of 1790 indicates, Bishop Auckland was inhabited by wealthy gentlemen and women, clergy, doctors, lawyers, as well as many traders and craftspeople. Joiners, glaziers, shoemakers, merchants, shopkeepers, linen drapers, blacksmiths and watchmakers were among those listed. In addition to these skilled workers, there is likely to have been a body of labourers or regular employees working alongside them. Although there was very little in the way of organised industry at this stage, there was a factory for printing calicos, muslins and cottons at West Mill, to the west of the town, operated by Messrs Scott & Company.

On High Bondgate, no. 28 (Greenback) is a good example of a modest, unpretentious two-storey house with a full-height canted bay window, and a relatively plain doorway and overlight suited to a modestly prosperous

Figure 20
Front elevation of no. 27 Market Place (The Elms),
viewed from the south.
[DP393014, Anna Bridson © Historic England Archive]

Figure 21
East elevation of no. 27 Market Place (The Elms).
[DP393016, Anna Bridson © Historic England Archive]

inhabitant. Another is no. 17 North Bondgate, which is a smaller two-storey house with a steeply pitched roof and narrow handmade bricks, which probably dates to the early 18th century (Fig. 22). It has stone copings and kneelers, and the windows have stone keystones and sills. On Fore Bondgate there are also examples of smaller, simple stone-built cottages, which were probably inhabited by the town's workers and their families.

Auckland Castle and parkland, together with the town's surviving 18th-century buildings, tell an important story about the reputation, status and development of Bishop Auckland at this time. Considerable investment by the bishops consolidated the exclusivity of the castle complex, which played a key role in the Durham bishopric. The town remained compact, but domestic buildings and public facilities flourished. Much of the built fabric of this period has not survived the test of time, with the vast growth of the 19th century resulting in many buildings being swept away, but what survives offers important insights into the social, commercial and domestic life of the town.

Figure 22
No. 17 North Bondgate, viewed from the north-west.
[DP290687, Alun Bull © Historic England Archive]

4

Industry and the expansion of the railway network

The 19th-century growth of mining in County Durham, coupled with the expansion of the regional railway network, stimulated the industrial development of Bishop Auckland. The town is situated within the southern limits of the Durham coalfield, an area which has been mined for its rich coal resources since the medieval period. In 1838 there were 14 coal pits within approximately 3 miles (about 5km) of the town, including a colliery in Bishop Auckland itself, located outside the south wall of Auckland Castle Park. Auckland coal was known for producing high-quality coke, which was greatly sought after by the iron and steel industry. The largest collieries within the area were Newton Cap (also known as Toronto), Woodhouse Close and Auckland Park. Many people living in the town were employed at these pits. By the 20th century, around 40 collieries operated within a radius of 5 miles (8km) around the town.

The first railway to Bishop Auckland was opened in 1843, as an extension of the Stockton and Darlington Railway (S&DR) from nearby Shildon (*see* facing page). This was followed by a further three major lines, which transformed Bishop Auckland into an important transport hub for both freight and passenger rail services. A railway station and goods station were located to the west of South Road (later Newgate Street) and the southern part of Bishop Auckland became increasingly industrialised, with a gas works and a brick and tile works established in this area, followed by a number of engineering companies. Bishop Auckland also had two flour mills. The Gaunless Roller Flour Mill on the bank of the River Gaunless, along Durham Chare, was set up in 1830 (Fig. 23). It was subsequently known as Ferens Flour Mill after Michael Ferens – elder brother of the Member of Parliament Thomas Robinson Ferens – who acquired the site in the 1870s. A second flour mill operated from West Mill, to the west of the town.

The development of the railways

The four major railway lines laid in Bishop Auckland from the mid-19th century onwards transformed the surrounding landscape with corridors of track, embankments, cuttings, bridges and viaducts. The first railway to Bishop Auckland was operated by the newly formed Bishop Auckland and Weardale Railway company (a subsidiary venture of the S&DR), which was authorised by an Act of Parliament on 15 July 1837.[23] The aim of this new line was to connect

Extract from the 6-inch Ordnance Survey map published in 1859 (surveyed 1857), showing the new railway lines and station at Bishop Auckland. [Reproduced with permission of the National Library of Scotland]

Figure 23
Aerial photograph, looking south, of the Ferens Mill
complex, taken by Aerofilms Ltd. in October 1950. The
mill, on Durham Chare, was destroyed by fire in 1970
and its site is now the entrance to the Willows.
[EAW033890 © Historic England Archive]

the Stockton and Darlington Railway with the coalfields around Crook and Howden-le-Wear to the north-west of Bishop Auckland, opening up access to coal reserves as well as other resources such as lime and stone.

The Bishop Auckland and Weardale Railway was overseen by Thomas Storey (1789–1859), formerly an engineer employed by George Stephenson (1781–1848); it took five years to build because of the complex engineering work involved. Shildon Tunnel (originally known as the Prince of Wales Tunnel) was built to carry the line north-westward towards Bishop Auckland. Completed in 1842, it runs 120ft (36.6m) below Shildon and cuts through a 500ft-high (approximately 152m) magnesian limestone ridge. The Holdforth Embankment Culvert was also built at Bishop Auckland to enable the railway to cross the River Gaunless, measuring approximately 0.5 miles (74m) long, 33ft (10m) in span, and 16ft (5m) high (Fig. 24). The 1857 Ordnance Survey map shows the line with the railway station to the west of what was previously South Road, together with an engine shed and goods station. A tunnel to the east of the station is also shown, but this was removed as the railway was expanded southwards.

In 1854, the North Eastern Railway started work on the line connecting Bishop Auckland to Durham, and thence to the London-Edinburgh route via the Leamside line. The route came into Bishop Auckland from the north, curved through land to the west of Newgate Street and South Road, and met the Bishop Auckland and Weardale line to the south. The engineer-in-chief was Thomas Elliot Harrison (1808–88) and the resident engineer was Robert Hodgson (1817–77), both prominent railway engineers with distinguished backgrounds. Three stone viaducts were needed along the route, including the Newton Cap Viaduct over the River Wear at Bishop Auckland, built between 1854 and 1857. It is around 828ft (252m) long with 11 semicircular arches, each with a span of

Figure 24
The southern portal of the Holdforth Embankment Culvert over the River Gaunless.
[Marcus Jecock © Historic England]

60ft (18m) (Fig. 25). The other two viaducts were built at Durham (Framwellgate North Road) and Belmont (Brasside) to a similar design. A tunnel had to be dug underneath High Bondgate and a bridge built at Princes Street (both since demolished) to carry the line southwards through the town. A road bridge was also built over the line to carry Tenters Street. The Durham to Bishop Auckland line was formally opened in April 1857. A temporary station was initially located on Tenters Street, although the main railway station on South Road (later Newgate Street) was enlarged to accommodate platforms for both the Bishop Auckland and Weardale line and the North Eastern Railway, which opened at the end of 1857.[24]

The North Eastern Railway also built two sets of four back-to-back cottages on the north side of High Bondgate, one to each side of the High Bondgate tunnel. Dating to the mid-19th century, they housed railway workers and are important as the only known cottages built by a railway company in Bishop Auckland (Fig. 26). Back-to-back cottages were common in the 19th century and were a cost-effective way of providing workers' housing. Urban examples were

Figure 25
Newton Cap Viaduct, viewed from Newton Cap Bridge located to the west.
[DP393081, Anna Bridson © Historic England Archive]

often economical on land and shared multiple party walls with neighbouring properties. This form of housing became associated with poor living conditions. The cottages built by the North Eastern Railway, however, appear to have been constructed to a higher standard in brick with stone details, with shared amenities in rear yards.

To the south and south-west of the town, the South Durham and Lancashire Union Railway line was extended to Bishop Auckland in 1863, having previously opened from Tebay in Cumbria (formerly Westmorland) to Barnard Castle (County Durham) in 1861. This line enabled the cross-regional transport of coke from south Durham to the ironworks of Cumbria, and Cumbrian iron ore to Teesside and Consett. To the east, the Bishop Auckland and Spennymoor Branch Railway line (later known as the Bishop Auckland and Ferryhill Railway) was opened in 1885 as an extension of the Byers Green Branch of the Clarence

Figure 26
Nos 46 and 48 High Bondgate, originally four back-to-back cottages built by the North Eastern Railway, viewed from the south.
[DP290686, Alun Bull © Historic England Archive]

Figure 27
The eastern elevation of the railway accommodation
bridge providing access beneath the line to retain a
connection between eastern parts of Auckland Castle
Park.
[Rebecca Pullen © Historic England]

Railway. This line ran directly through Auckland Castle Park, and a number of accommodation bridges had to be constructed in order to retain access between sections of the park and the surrounding farmland that were bisected by the imposed embankments and cuttings (Fig. 27). Bishop Lightfoot, who was in office at the time, requested that the bridge carrying the driveway to Auckland Castle over the new line should be built wide enough so that he could not see the railway, which he considered a blot on his landscape, when travelling by road between Bishop Auckland and Durham.

By the end of the 19th century, the town's railway station and goods station occupied a large area of land between what was previously South Road and the North Eastern Railway line (Fig. 28). The railway station was by this time a distinctive triangular shape serving the complicated network of lines that ran through it. The goods station was reorganised in the 1870s and a large shed was built for the loading and unloading of goods. The goods yard was extensive, accommodating sidings and cranes as well as a weighing machine. Over this towered the north junction signal box, co-ordinating rail traffic through this very busy intersection (Fig. 29).

Figure 28
Extract from the 1897 Ordnance Survey 25-inch map
(revised 1896), showing the railway lines, railway
station and goods yard in the southern part of Bishop
Auckland.

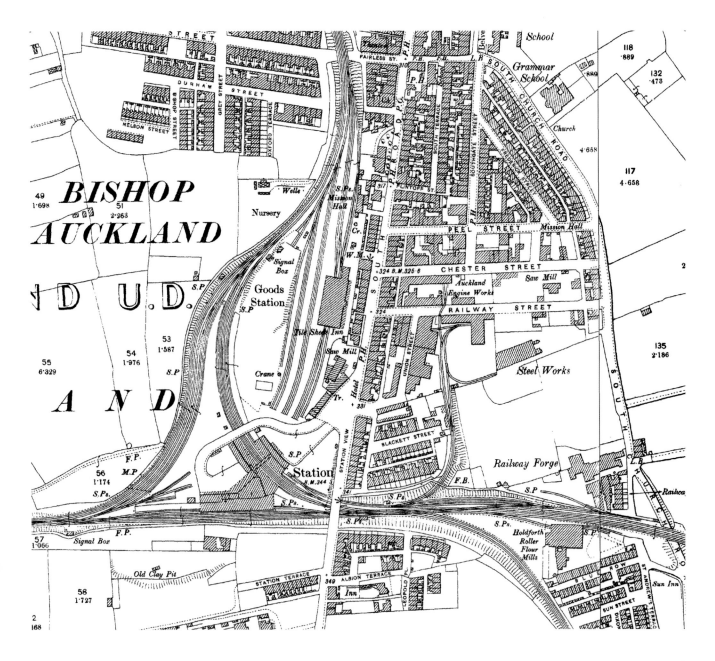

Figure 29
Bishop Auckland goods yard in 1970, with the north junction signal box in the background.
[Reproduced with kind permission of Ernie's Railway Archive]

The industrialisation of South Road (later Newgate Street)

From the early to mid-19th century onwards, the southern part of Bishop Auckland grew into a vibrant neighbourhood bustling with the occupants and employees of new housing and industrial ventures (Fig. 30). A long row of single-storey dwellings known as Brougham Place was built to the west side of South Road, and the open land to the east of the road, ripe for redevelopment, was subdivided into smaller plots for sale to new investors. Such opportunities did not escape the notice of Thomas Storey, who had been involved in forming the Bishop Auckland and Weardale Railway (*see* p. 38). He bought a piece of

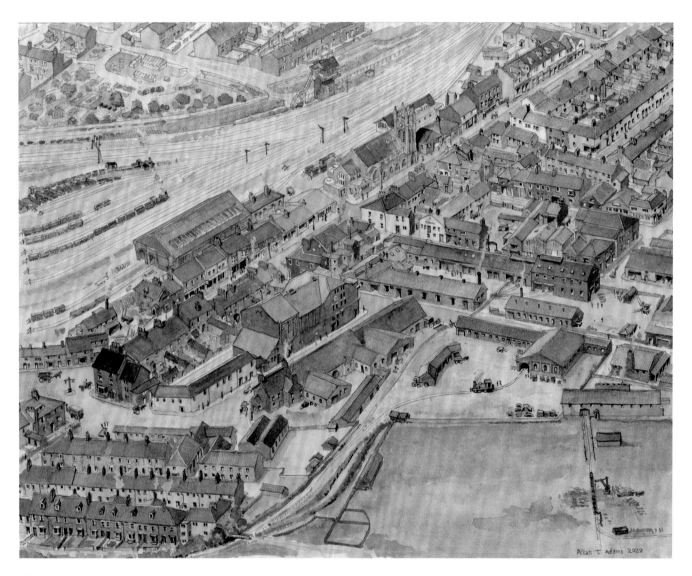

Figure 30
Reconstruction drawing of the South Road (later
Newgate Street) area of Bishop Auckland, about 1920.
[© Allan Adams, 2020/ © Historic England]

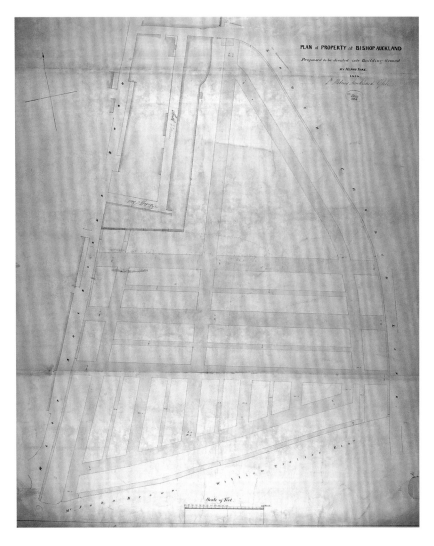

PLAN of PROPERTY at BISHOP AUCKLAND

Proposed to be divided into Building Ground

BY HENRY TUKE

Figure 31
'Plan of Property at Bishop Auckland, Proposed to be divided into Building Ground', by Henry Tuke, 1856. Tuke was a local businessman who descended from a York Quaker family.
[DUL CCB MP 511 Reproduced by permission of Church of England Record Centre/Durham University Library]

land and built a row of terraced houses on Flintoff Street in 1842, which he named after his married daughter, Hannah Flintoff. A proposed new layout for several streets to the south of Flintoff Street was made in 1856.[25] This was used as the basis for the construction of Peel Street, Chester Street, Railway Street,

Southgate Street and Frederick Street, the skeleton on which the new industrial community was formed (Fig. 31).

Three main engineering companies specialising in products for the railway and coal mining industries developed their business here: Lingford Gardiner & Company (established in 1861), the Auckland Ironworks (opened in 1863) and Robert Wilson & Sons (established 1842). In September 1856, Lingford Gardiner & Co acquired a plot of land between Railway Street and Chester Street which, over the course of 50 years, expanded to cover a site of 3 to 4 acres (about 1.4ha) that was served by its own railway spur, with a level crossing at Railway Street. They specialised in the repair and manufacture of locomotives for collieries and ironworks, as well as colliery hauling engines, winding engines, pit-head gear, points and crossings, gauges, steam boilers, brass fittings, castings and parts. The firm was run by Samuel Lingford and brothers George and John Gardiner. Samuel Lingford had other business ventures in Bishop Auckland. He ran a successful grocery store with his brother Joseph in Newgate Street, where they also began to make and sell baking powder. By 1888 the Lingford family had opened a factory dedicated to making baking powder in Durham Street.

Although greatly altered, the former premises of Lingford Gardiner & Co still stand on the south side of Railway Street and the east side of Union Street, and in the block between Chester Street and Railway Street. The company submitted a series of building applications to the council during the 1860s, which show some of the earliest buildings in this complex, and how they were used. A building application of 1868 outlined proposed plans for a 'Lathe Shop' to the south of Chester Street and a 'Smith's Shop' to the north of Railway Street. To the west of the 'Smith's Shop' was the 'Foundry'.[26] The proposed buildings were simple, single-storey brick structures with regularly spaced windows to allow plenty of light into the interior (Fig. 32). The smith's shop was open-sided to the north and had three furnaces with chimneys to the south. This plot was subsequently reorganised, but it is possible that some of these buildings, or parts thereof, were incorporated into the surviving complex. In a better condition are the company's structures to the south of Railway Street, which take the form of a series of linked one- and two-storey red-brick buildings with recessed panels, segmental-headed window openings and dog-tooth courses (Fig. 33). The central bay of the two-storey building has a wider opening at ground-floor level and a gable with stone coping, perhaps marking a main entrance.

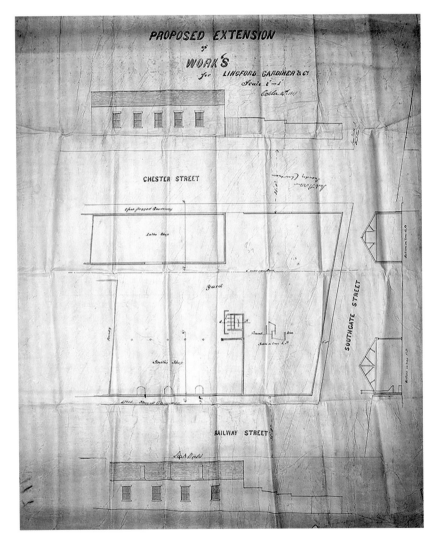

Figure 32
Building application for the extension of Lingford
Gardiner's works in Railway Street and Chester Street,
1868.
[UD/BA 432/99 Reproduced by permission of Durham
County Record Office]

By 1894, the Lingford Gardiner & Co site included iron and brass foundries, machine and fitting shops, engine erecting shops, a pattern shop and store, forges and a boiler shop. In the 1890s they also expanded into the manufacture and design of bicycles, patenting a model called the Rational Umpire Spring

Framed Cycle. The company operated until 1931, but prior to this their building to the east side of Union Street was already in alternative use as a drill hall, as shown on the 1920 Ordnance Survey map.

The Auckland Ironworks (later Auckland Steel Works) was built on a plot next to Lingford Gardiner & Co, on the south side of Railway Street. It was opened in 1863 by Joseph Vaughan, nephew of John Vaughan of the Middlesbrough-based Bolckow and Vaughan mining and iron-making company, initially to make edge tools and later as an ironworks. When it closed in 1884, part of the site was taken over by Lingford Gardiner. Another engineering firm, Robert Wilson & Sons, operated in this area. Although the business was established in 1842, it is not shown on the 1857 Ordnance Survey map, which suggests that it only began manufacturing here during the second half of the 19th century. In 1894 it was described as 'engineers, steel manufacturers, iron brass founders and forgemen, operating from Railway Forge and Auckland Steel Works', having also expanded into part of the former Auckland Ironworks site.[27] It also took over some of Lingford Gardiner & Co's business when it closed in 1931, and became a key employer in Bishop Auckland, operating until the 1990s.

Figure 33
Former premises of Lingford Gardiner on the south side of Railway Street, viewed from the south-east.
[DP393064, Anna Bridson © Historic England Archive]

Figure 34
The single-storey brick buildings along Railway Street
still give this area its industrial feel and many are still
used by manufacturing companies today.
[34095_018, Emma Trevarthen, 2018,
© Historic England Archive]

The regional importance of Bishop Auckland as a railway hub in the 19th and early 20th centuries, along with the rapid development of industry in the southern part of the town, had a lasting impact on Bishop Auckland. Today, Peel Street, Railway Street and Chester Street still retain their industrial 'feel', lined by many low-rise industrial buildings from the 19th and 20th centuries; these are occupied by independent garages, warehouses and commercial businesses (Fig. 34). In particular, the surviving structures of Lingford Gardiner & Co – although rather unassuming – have local importance because they are a reminder of the town's proud engineering past.

5

The expansion of Bishop Auckland from the mid-19th century

Bishop Auckland experienced a period of intense investment, rebuilding and expansion once the railways were established, with widespread industrial growth within and around the town. From the middle of the 19th century, a range of buildings was constructed to house, educate and support the burgeoning population, providing work spaces, shops and venues for refreshment and entertainment.

By 1857, the town had expanded south along Newgate Street beyond what is now known as Princes Street and new roads were laid out to the east and west of Newgate Street, including William Street (now the site of the Newgate Shopping Centre) and Tenters Street. Ordnance Survey maps published in 1857 and 1897 show the town centre packed with notable public buildings, religious institutions, schools, public houses and hotels (*see* facing page).

The power of the bishops, once so central to the town's identity and development, was diminishing. The bishops continued to hold many of their rights and property until 1836 when their powers were reduced by the Durham (County) Palatine Act and some of their authority passed to the Crown.[28] The Local Board of Health was established in 1854 in response to issues relating to the poor living conditions highlighted by inspections under the Public Health Act of 1848. Its successor was the Bishop Auckland Urban District Council under the Local Government Act of 1894, which also saw the amalgamation of the township of Pollards Lands with Bishop Auckland.

Public buildings

The market place remained the focal point for the town and saw much renewal. The Church of St Anne, standing at its heart, was built as a chapel of ease in the Early English style between 1845 and 1848 to the designs of William Thompson, as architect to the Ecclesiastical Commissioners (Fig. 35). It is fairly compact, with a nave, chancel, south aisle, vestry and porch. Adjacent to the church, a row of four almshouses first constructed in 1662 for two poor men and two poor women was rebuilt in 1845 and funded by Bishop Maltby. They are constructed of sandstone with slate roofs in a Tudor style, probably reflecting some of their predecessors' appearance.

Extract from the 1897 Ordnance Survey 25-inch map (surveyed in 1896) showing Bishop Auckland as a well-established market town.

Bishop Auckland was fortunate in having a well-established family of architects who were responsible for the design of a large proportion of its buildings in the second half of the 19th century and the early 20th century. William Thompson (c. 1810–58) was the architect of St Anne's (see p. 53) and was the father of William Vickers Thompson (1836–88) and Robert Wilkinson Thompson (1850–96). W. V. Thompson followed his father into the position of architect to the Ecclesiastical Commissioners, which he undertook alongside his private commissions. He was also later a member of the Local Board of Health. His notable works include the first phase of the Co-operative building (no. 80 Newgate Street) built in 1873–4, later extended in the same style in 1882–3 by his brother Robert. Other important buildings by W. V. Thompson included the former Royal George Hotel at the corner of Victoria Avenue (nos 41, 43 and 45 Newgate Street) and the Congregational Church at the corner of Regent Street and Kingsway built in 1877 (since demolished). He was also responsible for some of the houses along Victoria Avenue built in the 1870s and 1880s.

R. W. Thompson designed the Mechanics Institute on Victoria Avenue, completed in 1880–1, and the nearby Lightfoot Institute on Kingsway which was built as the Young Men's Church Institute in 1882. He also designed houses, including the Old Vicarage on Park Street which overlooks the River Gaunless, built about 1880. His son, Robert Brown Thompson (1878–1929), was responsible for a number of changes to existing buildings in and around the town including the additional storey at no. 25 Newgate Street (formerly McIntyre's boot and shoe shop).

Figure 35
The Church of St Anne in the market place, drawn by Reverend J W Hick in 1846. The church was designed by William Thompson as architect to the Ecclesiastical Commissioners. This view is not too dissimilar from that today, but shows houses on the site which is now occupied by the Town Hall, built in 1861–2.
[DCO Prints © Rut/Durham 4/37a Reproduced by permission of Durham County Record Office]

Prior to the mid-19th century, formal meetings to conduct town business were held in public houses, assembly rooms and hotels, but there was a greater need for dedicated meeting space once the Local Board of Health was established. The Bishop Auckland Town Hall and Market Company was duly formed as a joint stock company led by Colonel Henry Stobart (1795–1866), proprietor of Etherley Colliery and a director of the Stockton and Darlington Railway. The unusual multipurpose town hall combined a covered market, shops and Turkish baths on the ground floor with offices and lecture rooms above. It was built in the market place between 1861 and 1862 to the designs of John Philpott Jones (1830–73), amended by John Johnstone (1818–84) who also oversaw its construction.[29] It is a fine and imposing building built in the Gothic Revival style with northern French and Flemish influences. It continues to dominate the market place today and currently houses the town's central library as well as a café, meeting rooms and exhibition space (Fig. 36).

The rise of nonconformism, particularly Methodism, in the second half of the 19th century saw a number of new places of worship built across the town. The earliest of these was the Friends Meeting House at the corner of Great Gates and Newgate Street, which had a large accompanying burial ground. The 17th-century meeting house was rebuilt in 1840 and again in 1876, but it has since been demolished. Elsewhere, only fragmentary remains of the former Wesleyan Methodist Church – comprising now-rendered brick walls – survive in the eastern elevation of no. 56 North Bondgate; this was built in 1804, rebuilt in 1842 and rebuilt again in 1866. It was replaced by a new church in Newgate Street (formerly South Road), built in 1908–14 to the designs of the London-based architects Henry Thomas Gordon (1846–1922) and Josiah Gunter (1861–1930) at a cost of approximately £12,000.[30] Constructed in a Gothic Revival style using rock-faced stone with ashlar dressings, and with a tall tower accommodating a clock on each of its four sides (hence its current name, The Four Clocks Centre), the building acts as a key landmark within the north–south axis of the town (Fig. 37).

As to schools, the Barrington School, built about 1810 on the south side of the market place, provided mixed education for children until 1855 when the National School for girls and infants was opened. The National School was the first of three schools constructed on South Church Road during this period, an

Figure 36
The town hall, built in 1862, dominates this part of the market place. The Church of St Anne accompanies it to the south and the two turrets are complemented by the modern Auckland Tower in the background.
[DP290651, Alun Bull © Historic England Archive]

Figure 37
The former Wesleyan Methodist Church, Newgate
Street, now the Four Clocks Centre, built 1908–14.
[DP393025, Anna Bridson © Historic England Archive]

area of the town where educational provision has grown and remains prominent (Fig. 38). Thereafter, the Barrington School became an establishment for boys only and the School of Industry for girls on Silver Street (established in 1815 by Bishop Barrington) was closed. The National School was built on a T-shaped plan with separate wings and yards for juniors and infants. It was extended in about 1873 with a new north-east wing to the design of W. V. Thompson, and again between 1896 and 1898 with a new building to the south-east, later known as St Anne's School, by Frederick Clark (1854–1944) and William Jobson Moscrop (1858–1929). The whole complex was demolished between 2019 and 2022.

Figure 38
The King James I Grammar School (later the Lower School) on the right and the former National School beyond it to the left. This image is from an undated postcard.
[Pat Robbins]

King James I Grammar School initially occupied a first-floor room within the Church of St Anne, but the rebuilding of the church forced the school to move to new premises on South Terrace in 1846. The school moved again when a new privately funded school building was constructed on a site adjacent to the National School on South Church Road in 1864 to a design by Thomas Austin of Newcastle (1822–67), extended between 1875 and 1878 by W. V. Thompson. It included accommodation for boarders and is therefore very different in design from the more standardised plan of the National School. As was typical for a building of this date, its stone façade and side elevations contrasted with the cheaper brick rear elevations and extensions. It fell into disrepair after an arson attack in 2007, and only the front part of the building has been saved; despite this, it continues to be an impressive addition to the streetscape as well as a key reminder of the old school.

With the development of the labour movement and increased workers' rights across Britain, Bishop Auckland, like so many industrial towns, saw an increase in institutions promoting education for working-class adults. The first of these was the Temperance Hall (used most recently as a masonic hall), built of stone in a Gothic Revival style at the corner of Victoria Street (later Victoria

Avenue) in 1875–7 to a design by James Garry of Hartlepool (1849–1918) (Fig. 39). It was used as a platform from which the Temperance Society could promote their principles, as well as a place to further adult education. It consisted of a committee room, Band of Hope room (for the children) and tea preparation room on the ground floor, with a large assembly room with gallery above.[31] Its neighbour, the Mechanics Institute, was built in 1880–1, while just around the corner the Young Men's Church Institute, later known as the Lightfoot Institute, was built in 1882 (Fig. 40). Both were designed by R. W. Thompson, but they are very different in style and design. The small but attractive Mechanics' Institute is an eclectic mixture of styles with arched windows and carved floral details. It included rooms for a live-in caretaker on the ground floor, a position which was filled by Matthew Richley, the author and historian who published *The History and Characteristics of Bishop Auckland* in 1872. Other rooms were used for billiards and recreation, a library and a reading room.[32] The Young Men's Church Institute is constructed of roughly coursed stone with tall mullioned and transomed windows and pointed gables in a Jacobean style. Inside the building there was a large hall, class and recreation rooms and a library containing 300 volumes.[33]

Figure 39
The two Gothic Revival buildings of the former Temperance Hall, latterly a masonic hall (nos 25 and 26), and the Mechanics Institute (no. 27 Victoria Avenue), viewed from the north-east.
[DP393034, Anna Bridson © Historic England Archive]

Figure 40
The Lightfoot Institute, formerly the Young Men's Church Institute, on Kingsway, opened in 1882; viewed from the south-west.
[DP393040, Anna Bridson © Historic England Archive]

Commercial activity

Commerce remained centred on the market place in the 19th century, which is evident today in the rich architecture of the surviving buildings of that period, its preserved extent and its layout. A new market hall was required after the reconstruction of the Church of St Anne (completed in 1848), having formerly been located in the base of the earlier church's tower. Thus, a small detached market hall (known as the Market Cross), providing shelter for market sellers and incorporating a public pant (water fountain), was built in the centre of the market place in about 1848, not far from the west front of the new church. It was described by Fordyce in 1855 as octagonal in plan and constructed of polished stone with open sides, crenellated roof and cupola (or lantern). Like the church, it was designed by William Thompson. Sadly, it fell into a poor state of repair and was demolished in about 1859, just before work started on the new town hall, which itself precipitated a wave of investment within the market place.

Banks, shops, refreshment houses and hotels lined the market place, overlooking the new town hall. This commercial activity spilled out onto Newgate Street and Fore Bondgate. The earliest purpose-built bank was the Bishop Auckland Savings Bank (now the Mining Art Gallery, no. 45 Market Place) constructed on the east side of the Church of St Anne in about 1860 (altered in 1870) in dressed stone with an interesting circular turret. It was amalgamated with the Backhouse & Company Bank in 1870, which opened new premises in 1871 on the opposite side of the market place (no. 2 Market Place). The tall, three-storey building, constructed in brick with stone dressings in an eclectic style, was designed by G. G. Hoskins (1837–1911) and is one of the most striking buildings within the market place today (Fig. 41). The bank was merged with Barclays in 1896 and is now part of the Spanish Gallery. Other banks of a more modest appearance included the York City & County Bank (no. 21 Newgate Street) constructed in 1893 to the designs of Walter H. Brierley (1862–1926) and James Demaine (1842–1911) of York, and the Yorkshire Penny Bank (no. 18 Newgate Street) built on the opposite side of the street in 1898 to the designs of John R. Whitaker (1872–1944) of Leeds.[34] The eclectic and polychromatic York City & County Bank was originally faced with stone at ground level and with red brick above (now replaced with granite) (Fig. 42).[35] In contrast, the Yorkshire Penny Bank is constructed of dressed stone in a mixture of baronial, Tudor and

Figure 41
The south side of the market place showing the former Backhouse & Company Bank, built 1871, in the centre. Hedley's drapery store (later Doggarts) was located in the classical building on its right side.
[DP290645, Alun Bull © Historic England Archive]

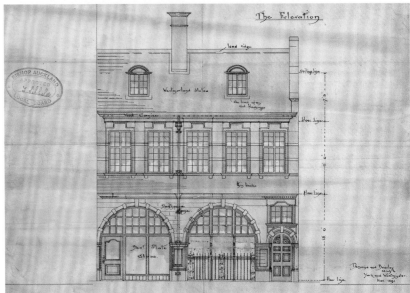

Figure 42
The front elevation of the York City & County Bank on Newgate Street, as proposed in 1891.
[UD/BA 432/309 Reproduced by permission of Durham County Record Office]

Elizabethan styles (*see* Fig. 47). The corner turret dominates this area of Newgate Street and incorporates its construction date (1898) and the date when the Yorkshire Penny Bank was established (1859).

Before about 1870, most of the shops were of a modest scale and were often originally built as houses with an adapted room at the front for sales. In addition to stores at the back or above, some also had outbuildings, stables and workshops in a yard at the rear, often reached by a passageway from the front. Surviving examples on Fore Bondgate and Newgate Street take this form. Historical directories in the second half of the 19th century list a range of specialist shops and trades including linen and woollen drapers, hatters, curriers (leather workers) and metalworkers (tin, iron and brass), as well as grocers, bakers and fishmongers. There was a large number of butchers' shops serving the expanding town and surrounding area, presumably relating to the auction mart located off Tenters Street (now the site of the bus station). A fine example of a specialist shop dating from the mid- to late 19th century is at nos 103 and 105 Newgate Street. It was built as a butcher's shop with slaughterhouse to the rear and was occupied by the Gregory family from at least 1871, eventually growing to include a beef shop on one side and a pork shop on the other (Fig. 43).

Figure 43
A photograph of Gregory & Sons butchers, nos 103 and 105 Newgate Street, taken in the early 1900s before the shopfront was renewed.
[© the Gregory family]

Many of the people living and working within Bishop Auckland in the second half of the 19th century had relatively low incomes. Consequently, the shops remained small-scale in order to be affordable for their customers, although the arrival of the co-operative movement, first established in Rochdale in 1844, was to change this. Members of the co-operative were given shares based on their purchases and the shared capital was used to buy wholesale goods which could then be sold at affordable prices. The first co-operative shop in Bishop Auckland was established in a house on Belvedere (South Church Road, later Kingsway) in 1860, but the business soon grew and moved to alternative premises on Newgate Street in 1862. This building was replaced in 1873 by a rather grand three-storey building with stone façade and Gothic Revival details (no. 80 Newgate Street). It was designed by W. V. Thompson and comprised grocery and shoe and boot departments, stabling and warehousing. It was extended to the south in 1882–3 in a similar style by R. W. Thompson. In 1902 the co-operative also acquired the neighbouring premises, originally built

Figure 44
The imposing three-storey row of the former Co-operative Central Stores at no. 80 Newgate Street, viewed from the south-east.
[DP290678, Alun Bull © Historic England Archive]

in 1894.[36] The four phases of development can be identified by date stones along the parapet of the front elevation, although these are slightly earlier than the documented completion dates, and by a sequence of vertical straight joints in the stonework, particularly between the 1894 building at the south end and the three phases to the right of it (Fig. 44).

By the early 1870s, larger shops and emporiums were beginning to appear in Bishop Auckland, including Hedley's drapery emporium (then Doggarts from 1895) located on the south side of Market Place. The building was extended and refronted between 1871 and 1874 with a new three-storey classical stone façade which reflects the growing commercial confidence in the town at the time (*see* Fig. 41).[37] The shop included sales space on the first floor with the large segmental arched windows at the front providing plenty of light by which shoppers could view the merchandise. Victoria Street (later Victoria Avenue) was also laid out in the early 1870s, its western end framed by the three-storey, classical-style buildings of Victoria House (on its south side) and the Royal George Hotel (on the north side). Victoria House was built as Cleminson's colossal furniture emporium and became Burton's tailors in the 1920s. The Royal George was described in *The Yorkshire Post and Leeds Intelligencer* in August 1876 as one of the largest hotels in the town, containing a dining room, coffee room, sitting room, smoke room, commercial room and 50 bedrooms, with stabling for 30 horses, coach houses and a lawn behind. Around the same time, the row of buildings on the western side of Newgate Street (nos 30, 32, 34 and 36, which included the Black Horse Inn, the Red Lion Hotel and three shops) between Tenters Street and William Street (now occupied by the Newgate Shopping Centre) were rebuilt as the street was widened following proposals by the Local Board.[38] The block is a prominent three-storey row, constructed in stone. On the opposite side of the street, Central Buildings (nos 37 and 39), another three-storey building with shops on the ground floor and accommodation above, was added in 1885. It is relatively ornate with its mansard roof, round-headed dormer windows, moulded window surrounds with shaped pediments and carved motifs, and projecting first-floor windows.

Commercial activity was thriving at the beginning of the 20th century and many shops had their building façades, shopfronts and interiors renovated (Fig. 45). The double shopfront of Gregory's butchers (*see* p. 66) was added in about 1910. It has a deeply splayed central lobby with a

Figure 45
Market Place in about 1912 showing some of the larger
shops and emporiums and the commercial vibrancy
within the town centre. The Talbot Inn can be seen at
the top of Fore Bondgate with its distinctive corner
turret.
[Pat Robbins]

mirrored soffit. The shop window of no. 105 (Gregory's bakers) is framed by wooden pilasters and incorporates stained glass with the name 'GREGORY' picked out in white (Fig. 46). The interior was probably also refurbished at this time, including the colourful tiles depicting countryside scenes featuring cows and sheep. Similarly, the surviving shop window of the former Finlay's watchmakers and jewellery shop (no. 102), with attractive foliate details at the corners of the glass, demonstrates that smaller businesses were also doing well at this date.

Figure 45
Market Place in about 1912 showing some of the larger shops and emporiums and the commercial vibrancy within the town centre. The Talbot Inn can be seen at the top of Fore Bondgate with its distinctive corner turret.
[Pat Robbins]

22019   GENERAL VIEW LOOKING EAST, BISHOP AUCKLAND.

Figure 46
Gregory's butchers at no. 105 Newgate Street is a fine
example of a well-preserved shop front dating from
about 1910.
[DP290667, Alun Bull © Historic England Archive]

A number of public houses, inns and hotels were built in Market Place, Fore Bondgate and Newgate Street in the late 19th and early 20th centuries. One of the leading hotels was the Talbot Inn which once stood on the site of no. 43 Market Place (*see* Fig. 45). Rebuilt in 1875 when the east end of Fore Bondgate was widened, it was a particularly large hotel built in a Gothic style with a prominent corner turret. It had a distinctive two-storey stable with space for carriages at ground level and stables for horses on the first floor accessed using a ramp. The wave of new commercial investment at the end of the 19th century and early 20th century is also demonstrated by the reconstructed Queen's Head (rebuilt in 1898) and the Bay Horse (rebuilt about 1909).[39] Both display a similar Arts and Crafts style and incorporate false timber framing in their front elevations.

With so much activity, it is unsurprising that parts of the town started to become congested, leading to further widening of the upper part of Newgate Street (*see* p. 64). One by one, the buildings on its western side, north of William Street (now Newgate Shopping Centre), were rebuilt and set back between 1898 and 1912. This row included the Yorkshire Penny Bank and the North Eastern Bank, along with three public houses: the Market Tavern, the Criterion Hotel

Figure 47
Nos 2–18 Newgate Street showing the range of buildings that were rebuilt, or partially rebuilt, between 1898 and 1910; viewed from the south-east. The former Yorkshire Penny Bank with its distinctive corner turret is located in the centre of the image, its neighbour to the right is the former Market Tavern, while on the far right the brick buildings were rebuilt as the White Lion Hotel. [DP290675, Alun Bull © Historic England Archive]

and the White Lion Hotel (Fig. 47). The Market Tavern (no. 14 and possibly also 16, previously the Spirit Vaults) was rebuilt about 1899. It was described in *The Durham County Advertiser* in September 1900 as 'newly rebuilt' with an elaborate tiled front (sadly gone) and comprising extensive bars, service areas, six bedrooms, stabling and a bottling warehouse with stores above. In 1899, a new façade was planned for the Criterion Hotel (no. 12) to the designs of Frederick Howard Livesay (*c* 1869–1924). The White Lion (nos 6 to 8) was entirely rebuilt with new stabling to the rear between 1911 and 1912.[40]

Housing

In common with many towns across Britain in the mid-19th century, Bishop Auckland contained some areas with very poor living conditions. Significant concerns were identified by a public health enquiry published in 1852 (and again in 1856), noting poor or absent drainage, a deficiency of privies and sanitation, insufficient and poor-quality water supplies and overcrowding. The key areas affected were Back Bondgate (later North Bondgate), Newgate Street and Townhead.

Back-to-back houses and lodging houses were common and were concentrated on Dial Stob Hill, Wear Chare, Finkle Street, Clayton Street, on the north side of North Bondgate, the east side of Newgate Street (formerly South Road), Flintoff Street and South Terrace. These houses were particularly small, with only a single room on the ground and first floors, and shared facilities within a communal yard. By the end of the century, many of these houses had either been replaced or amalgamated to create 'through houses' (two back-to-back houses knocked through to become one single larger house). A rare surviving example can be found at nos 31 and 32 South Terrace (*see* Fig. 78). This pair was originally a block of four back-to-back stone cottages, built on the plot directly behind nos 131 and 135 Newgate Street.

In stark contrast, there were much larger houses built in Bishop Auckland in the mid-19th century, although many have since been subdivided. An excellent example can be found in Newgate Street (nos 73 and 75): this was once a large three-storey house, known as Beethoven House, which ran through to Kingsway and had extensive gardens to the rear. It was home of the Brotherton family who had their music shop on the ground floor. A row of six similar three-storey houses (now amalgamated and converted into the Belvedere Club) is located at the corner of Kingsway and South Church Road, originally known as Belvedere.

The town increasingly attracted middle-class professionals and investors. To accommodate them, new larger terraced houses were built along Victoria Street (later Victoria Avenue) and Regent Street, and very large detached and paired villas were added along Park Street in the 1870s and 1880s, overlooking Durham Chare and the River Gaunless (Fig. 48). The front elevations of the Victoria Street houses are constructed of dressed stone, while most of the rear elevations and two-storey rear wings are constructed in red brick (others in stone), many

Figure 48
Nos 13–23 Victoria Avenue, viewed from the south-east.
[DP393042, Anna Bridson © Historic England Archive]

with attic gables in their pitched slate roofs. The back lanes behind the houses of Victoria Avenue retain their grey-blue scoria paving bricks, made in Darlington from blast-furnace slag. They were commonly used across much of the North East and Yorkshire in the late 19th and early 20th centuries. There are subtle differences between the houses, particularly in the design and size of windows and doors, which may reflect the status of their owners and the affordability of their construction. The imposing Park Street villas are set within sizeable plots, with the principal elevation on the east side facing a generous terraced garden and country views. Each has its own architectural embellishments, although they share a Gothic Revival idiom and are built of stone; their gables, decoratively slated roofs, bargeboards and an occasional turret bring variety to their rooflines.

Leisure and entertainment

For centuries, Auckland Castle and its park remained a place very much for the private use of the bishop, but in the early 19th century the inhabitants of the town were gradually allowed to visit the park for leisure. From the 1850s, the park hosted an annual horticultural fete (later known as the Annual Gala of the North), which grew to become one of the county's premier events, depicted in an 1860 oil painting by J. W. Carmichael (*Flower Show in Auckland Park, County Durham, 1859*) with an enormous throng of finely dressed spectators. By the 1890s, the park was open daily, and local gentry and professionals were permitted to ride their carriages through it during daylight hours.

Golf was played in the outer park from about 1890 onwards, notably by theological students training at the castle. It was not until 1894, however, that the Bishop Auckland Golf Club was established (with the bishop as the president) and a formal course was laid out, transforming a large part of the outer park known as the High Plain. The original 9-hole course was designed by James Kay (*c.* 1855–1927) and was extended to 18 holes in 1913–14. The first clubhouse was a former tennis pavilion relocated from the cricket ground. This was replaced in 1902 by a timber structure and an extension was added in 1909; the current brick clubhouse was constructed in 1969, further extended and improved in 1983.

A cricket ground was established on the eastern side of Kingsway in the mid-19th century, on land held by the bishops. In 1882, the ground was shared by the amateur football club formed by the Young Men's Church Institute, later reformed as the Auckland Town Football club in 1887 and again in 1893 as the Bishop Auckland Football Club. The club was extremely successful between 1893 and 1988, winning the Football Association Amateur Cup 10 times (they were the only club to win it 4 times in a row, between 1955 and 1957) and the league championship 19 times. The ground had a grandstand on its northern boundary in the late 19th century, now removed; the timber cricket pavilion built in 1903 to the designs of William Perkins (*c.* 1870–1908) survives.[41]

There was considerable economic development within Bishop Auckland between the mid-19th century and the early decades of the 20th century. This is expressed in a rich and varied architectural legacy, notably its public and commercial buildings, higher-class housing and the survival of the market place and Newgate Street at the historical core of the town. Some areas of the town retained a rural feel before this time and the area east of Kingsway and South Church Road continued to be agricultural land until the 1860s. This change from a rural to a more urban environment was felt not just locally but also regionally: Bishop Auckland was now a town servicing the influx of people drawn there by new work opportunities, moving to live there and on its outskirts.

6

The 20th century, a time of change

Bishop Auckland entered the 20th century as a thriving commercial centre, but there were turbulent times ahead (*see* facing page). The family-run firms and emerging new chain stores established in the 19th century and early 20th century on Newgate Street in particular continued to attract customers from near and far with a tempting array of products. Picture postcards and photographs show that the market was still a huge draw, with stall after stall crammed into the market place (Fig. 49). In 1969 *The Bishop Auckland Official Guide and Industrial Handbook* heralded it as 'without doubt, the principal shopping centre for the whole of south-west Durham'. The leisure industry was also flourishing, with theatres, cinemas and other forms of entertainment proving increasingly popular.

The contraction of the mining industry in the North East in the 1920s and 1930s, combined with the economic crash of 1929 and the subsequent Great Depression, brought huge change to industry and employment. Many pits in the surrounding areas closed and rail traffic also started to decline. These changes brought about a substantial rise in unemployment, reaching 80 per cent in nearby Jarrow (near Newcastle) and leading to the famous hunger march on London in 1936. This economic downturn, coupled with a programme of slum clearance by the Bishop Auckland Urban District Council from the late 1930s

Extract from the 1920 Ordnance Survey 25-inch (revised 1915) map showing the areas to the west of Newgate Street (north of Tenters Street) and north of North Bondgate prior to large-scale housing clearances.

Figure 49
A postcard showing a busy market day with stalls, vehicles and people packed into the market place, about 1950.
[Pat Robbins/Hallmark Cards]

onwards, meant that swathes of housing and familiar landmarks such as the railway and goods station were demolished to make way for new initiatives. In the second half of the century, the road network was reworked to accommodate and encourage cars into the town. Consumer habits also began to change, and the rise of supermarkets brought about a huge shift in the way in which people used the high street.

Shopping in the 1920s and 1930s

In the first few decades of the 1900s several businesses on Newgate Street expanded their premises and gave them a fresh new look, with striking shopfronts incorporating fashionable Art Deco designs. McIntyre's boot and shoe shop, operating from no. 25 Newgate Street since the early 1890s, was ambitiously remodelled in 1909, adding new workshops, stockrooms, and a new shop front (Fig. 50). It was raised by a storey over what had originally been two shops, new flat-fronted oriel windows with curved sides lit the first floor, and a florid pediment topped with a weathervane gave central emphasis to the roof. This design by Robert Brown Thompson allowed plenty of light into the upper storage areas and additional display space, as well as an area for painted signs between the windows. Later, the rear plot was completely overbuilt with workshops and stockroom spaces, leaving a small lightwell. In the 1930s the shopfront was also replaced, complementing the two renovated upper storeys (Fig. 51). It has two recessed entrances with mosaic floors flanked by curved plate-glass display windows. Simple Art Deco features were incorporated into the design, including bronze colonettes around the windows, a polished granite base and the oval in the fascia signage bearing the name 'McIntyre'. Many of these features are original, including the functioning awning with winding mechanism. Investment in their building was a bold statement of McIntyre's growing wealth and success, and confidence in the future of their business.

In 1922 Woolworths opened a new shop at no. 84 Newgate Street, their 116th store in the country. They were viewed by many town councils as a desirable new employer, and their shops were regarded as a great draw to the high street. The two-storey design is typical of their stores at this time of rapid

·Front·Elevation·

Figure 50
Proposed elevation of no. 25 Newgate Street with second-floor extension, designed by R. B. Thompson, 1909. The central pediment may have been executed in a more restrained style, or was altered at a later date. [UD/BA 432/1206 Reproduced with permission of Durham County Record Office]

Figure 51
The former Marks & Spencer and McIntyre's shop at nos 23 and 25 Newgate Street, viewed from the south-west. [DP234511, Alun Bull © Historic England Archive]

expansion, with a salesroom on the ground floor and a storeroom above. The upper floor has a run of five windows, capped with a cornice and stepped parapet; the central three windows break forward slightly, adding interest to the frontage. The store was modernised and reopened in December 1960 with a bold new shopfront boasting a bank of four metal-framed doors flanked by small display windows, known as 'see-through shopfronts' (Fig. 52).[42]

Figure 52
Exterior shop front of Woolworths, no. 84 Newgate Street, Bishop Auckland, 1960–1970. The store closed in 2008.
[FWW01/01/0116/001 © Historic England Archive]

In 1930 Marks & Spencer opened a new store at no. 23 Newgate Street, built in a prominent Art Deco style (Fig. 53 and *see* Fig. 51). They had operated in Bishop Auckland since 1911, and this new shop was a clear sign of certainty in their future. The tripartite first-floor window arrangement of the new store, separated by paired pilasters, is particularly distinctive of this well known high-street chain. The original shopfront, which partially survives, has a polished granite base, iron frame and curved glass. Doggarts, a department store with a large site on Market Place and Newgate Street, refronted nos 7 and 9 Newgate

Figure 53
Proposed new premises at Bishop Auckland for Messsrs Marks & Spencer Ltd, designed by George J. Bell, 1930.
[UD/BA 432/1659-1660 Reproduced with permission of Durham County Record Office]

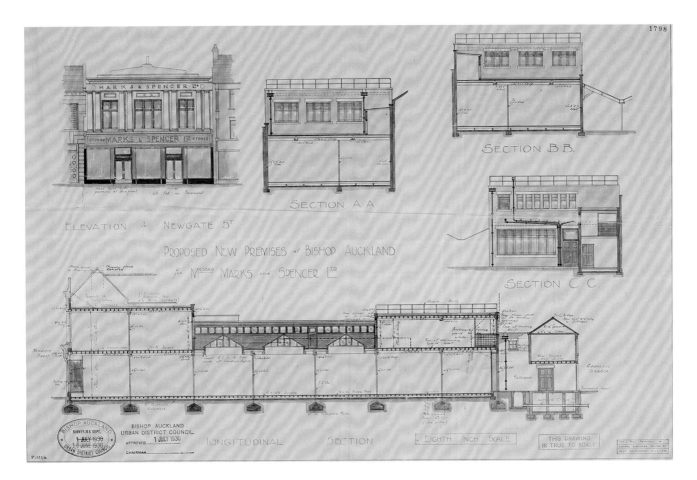

Figure 54
Nos 7 and 9 Newgate Street, part of the former Doggarts
department store, and linked to premises in the Market
Place.
[DP290661, Alun Bull © Historic England Archive]

Street with an Art Deco elevation almost identical to that of Marks & Spencer, with similar tripartite first-floor windows and paired pilasters (Fig. 54). Interspersed with the older commercial properties, these new and updated buildings on Newgate Street signalled that Bishop Auckland's high street was a modern, attractive place to shop.

Leisure and entertainment

At the turn of the 20th century theatres showing live performances were popular among the residents of the town. The long-established Eden Theatre, formerly the Masonic Music Hall constructed in 1865, reopened in 1892 at the corner of Newgate Street and Princes Street; it was run by Arthur Jefferson, father of the comic actor Stan Laurel. The Eden continued to show live performances until 1927, when it was converted into a cinema. In 1909, the Hippodrome Theatre in Railway Street was opened by managing director Signor Rino Pepi (1872–1927), an impresario who created a chain of music halls across northern England. It was designed by Darlington architect Joseph James Taylor (1881–unknown) under the supervision of George F. Ward of the Birmingham-based architectural firm Owen & Ward. Unable to compete with the growing demand for film, the theatre went into liquidation within less than two years of its opening and was converted to a Picton's Pictures cinema in 1912.[43]

The first purpose-built cinema was the King's Hall Picture House at no. 77 Newgate Street (Fig. 55). It was built in 1914 for G. W. Rudd to the designs of local architect Douglas Crawford and opened the following year. It was an innovative, mixed-use scheme which contained a curving 'Arcade' of five shops leading to the 'Picture Hall' at the rear of the plot, backing onto Kingsway. It showed silent films as well as having a stage for live variety performances, a library, ballroom and restaurant.[44] It was originally three storeys in height; the large oriel window lighting the first floor with its curved glass survives, as do the windowsills of the tall third floor, although the windows are now blocked, and the building has been reduced in height. It proved to be highly popular and later extended into a neighbouring building (no. 75, formerly Beethoven House). Its location, joining the group of new, fashionable shops opened on Newgate Street in the first decades of the century, must have contributed to its success. The now-demolished Majestic, on Tenters Street, was the last purpose-built cinema constructed in the town. It opened in 1939 and, with 1,385 seats and a wide screen of 40ft (12m), had the capacity to show films on a large scale. In 1944 it became part of the Odeon Cinemas chain and was renamed the Odeon in 1946.

The Olympia Skating Rink on the north side of Railway Street (the plot now occupied by no. 6 Railway Street) offered an alternative form of entertainment from 1909 (Fig. 56), when it was advertised as 'The Finest Skating Rink Surface

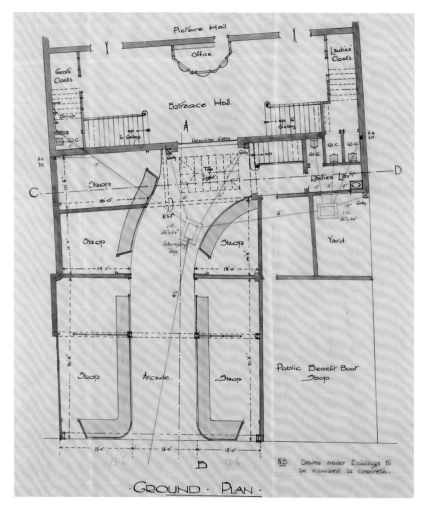

Figure 55
Proposed plans for the Arcade Picture House, Newgate Street, Bishop Auckland, designed by Douglas Crawford, August 1914.
[UD/BA 432/1361 Reproduced with permission of Durham County Record Office]

in the District' with a rock maple floor, four roller skating sessions a day, a café serving afternoon teas, and music provided by a military band.[45] Demonstrations were given by a Professor P. Hall, 'the World's Renowned Teacher of Scientific and Ornamental Skating' at the end of each session. By 1912 it also operated as a music hall and hosted Saturday-night boxing matches. It later became a billiard hall and then a motor garage, but has now been demolished.[46]

Figure 56
Proposed plan of the roller skating rink for The
Olympia Rink Company Ltd, Railway Street, Bishop
Auckland, designed by James Garry, 1909.
[UD/BA 432/1210 Reproduced with permission of
Durham County Record Office]

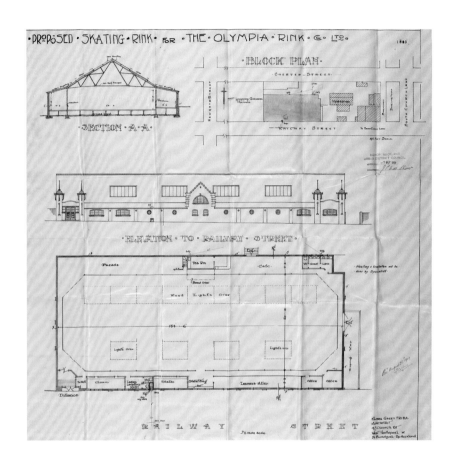

Schools

In 1929 the Barrington School at no. 3 Market Place was enlarged and
remodelled to the designs of Douglas Crawford after it received a generous
donation from a former pupil, Sir John Priestman (1855–1951), a shipbuilder
who made a fortune from investments in South African goldmines (Fig. 57).[47]
He is known for his endowment of local schools, churches (including St Andrew,
Roker by E. S. Prior), libraries and the Sunderland Technical College (now the
University of Sunderland). The ashlar front of the Barrington School stands out

in the market place against the older 18th- and 19th-century buildings. In 1974 the school moved to Woodhouse Lane and is now known as Bishop Barrington Academy.

The Bishop Auckland County Girls' School is the largest and the most impressive of the schools built along South Church Road, the others being St Anne's (National School) built in 1855, King James I Grammar School built 1865 and King James I Academy added in 2014 (*see* Chapter 5). It was designed in 1910 by Edwin Francis Reynolds (1875–1949) of Birmingham for 270 girls, with laboratories and a gymnasium (Fig. 58). A new west wing was started in 1939 although it was not completed until 1954, having been delayed by the Second World War (the area to the north of the school also accommodated a large number of air raid shelters), housing a new dining room and kitchen. The

Figure 57
The former Barrington School on the left and the former Backhouse & Co Bank on the right, now the Spanish Gallery.
[DP290649, Alun Bull © Historic England Archive]

school's interior retains much of its original layout, fixtures and fittings, including doors, stair handrails and tiling and remains in use today.

The schools along Kingsway and South Church Road form a close network of educational buildings. In 1962 the King James I Grammar School for boys (located in its 1864 building) and Bishop Auckland County Girls' School were amalgamated as the Bishop Auckland Grammar School. The King James I Grammar School continued to be used as the Lower School until 1992. The grammar school became a comprehensive in 1974, and new buildings were added to the south-east of the site in 1976. The 1976 buildings were subsequently demolished and replaced with a new building and the school was renamed King James I Academy in 2014.

Industry

The depression in world trade during the 1920s and 1930s severely affected industry in the north-east of England. Pits in the south-west Durham coalfield around Bishop Auckland either closed completely or reduced the number of employees, causing unemployment to soar. Local firms closed, including Lingford Gardiner & Co, an engineering company which supplied heavy industry (*see*

Chapter 4). It was reported in the 1954 *Urban District of Bishop Auckland Official Guide* that 68 per cent of all men in the town in 1932 were unemployed, and there were few opportunities for employment for women. The former Employment Exchange on Kingsway, built in about 1925 to a design by the Office of Works, still stands as a testimony to those bleak days (Fig. 59). Some drift mining and open-cast mining restarted in the 1940s, and older flooded mines were pumped out and temporarily reopened. By the end of the 1960s, however, all the deep mines in the south-west Durham coalfield were permanently closed.

The decline in the coal industry, coupled with a drop in Weardale lead, ironstone and limestone production, strongly affected the volume of rail traffic passing through Bishop Auckland. The introduction of regular bus services and the increased popularity of cars also began to influence the demand for passenger services. The railways experienced a short revival during the Second World War, but this was not enough to secure their long-term future. Nearly all the lines through the town were closed as part of the national rationalisation of the railway network in the 1950s and 1960s, cutting long-established passenger rail links to Barnard Castle, Durham, Crook, Spennymoor and Ferryhill. Apart from passenger services to Darlington, the only other remaining services by 1966 were those to the disposal site at Etherley Station and to the cement works at Eastgate. Some, but not much, freight capability was maintained.

Just as the arrival of the railways had such a dramatic impact on the development of the town, so too did their closure. Miles of track, tunnels, bridges

Figure 59
The former Employment Exchange on Kingsway, built in about 1925.
[DP393050, Anna Bridson © Historic England Archive]

and other railway infrastructure became obsolete and the goods yard and goods station to the south of the town closed by the end of 1971. This large site became derelict, and demolition began in 1981. The Newton Cap Viaduct, a prominent and long-standing local landmark, was also now redundant.

Housing and infrastructure

In the early 20th century, changes were made to the road network in order to improve access into and around the town. The earliest of these was Durham Road, which opened to traffic in 1929 and provided a route directly into the market place at its south-western corner, bypassing Durham Chare for the first time (Fig. 60). This required the removal of around a quarter of the walled gardens on the western boundary of Auckland Castle Park and a small area of woodland at the north end of Castle Chare.

This was followed by the large-scale clearance of areas of substandard housing. National recognition of poor housing conditions, particularly after the First World War, led to a series of acts which gave local authorities powers to demolish and replace low-quality housing. In 1939, under the Housing Act of

Figure 60
An undated postcard showing Durham Chare to the left and the new Durham Road bypass to the right.
[Pat Robbins/Hallmark Cards]

1936, the Urban District Council ordered the clearance of properties across the town in Gregory's Yard (to the east of Newgate Street, behind nos 103 and 105), Market Place, Jock's Row, Clayton Street, George Street (where the bus station is now located), Finkle Street and Silver Street. The yards of tiny, tightly packed houses behind properties on the north side of North Bondgate were also targeted by this programme. While this was underway, the western end of North Bondgate was widened to improve the traffic flow from High Bondgate, which involved demolishing buildings and cutting back several plots on both the north and south sides of the street.

In 1945 the council embarked on an ambitious new house-building scheme, with the aim of constructing 1,698 houses in the Bishop Auckland urban area to accommodate households displaced by slum clearance.[48] This included temporary prefabricated bungalows in Bishop Auckland, and houses and bungalows in West Auckland, St Helen's Auckland, Leeholme and Coundon. A total of 1,200 new houses were planned for the new housing estate at Woodhouse Close in the south of Bishop Auckland, which comprised municipal and private housing. By the end of 1953, around half of the proposed new houses had been built, vastly improving the housing conditions for a significant proportion of the population, particularly those who were less affluent. It also marked a change in the composition of the town, with fewer people living in the historic core and an increasing level of separation between the areas where people lived and worked.

During the 1950s and 1960s, additional areas of housing were cleared following the New Towns Act of 1946 and the publication of Durham County Council's Development Plan in 1951. Further properties on Finkle Street were demolished, along with houses on Saddler Street, Tenters Street and the yards behind the eastern side of Newgate Street, plus Wear Chare, The Batts, Jock's Row and Dial Stob Hill. In 1977, a huge area between High Bondgate/Finkle Street and Tenters Street, including Clayton Street, George Street, Saddler Street, Thompson Street and Grainger Street was demolished, containing substandard housing as well as buildings such as the Edgar Memorial Hall of 1883. Two years later, the Bishop Auckland Town Action Plan of 1979 published by Wear Valley District Council set out a proposal for a large central bus station in this area alongside improved vehicular access into the town, with the aim of reducing congestion and drawing in new investment. It was also where the tall multistorey office block for the Department of Health and Social Security (now known as Vinovium House) was built in 1969–71 (Fig. 61). Although controversial for its size and Brutalist style, it brought much needed new employment to the area.

The former route of the Bishop Auckland to Durham railway line was converted into a new urban bypass road which opened in 1980 to relieve traffic along Newgate Street. Reusing historic infrastructure in this way was a clever decision that allowed traffic to flow quite comfortably around the old town with less intrusion than similar new bypasses elsewhere. Nonetheless, it involved the demolition of two bridges, at Princes Street and Tenters Street, the latter replaced with a footbridge. The road was named after Bob Hardisty (1921–86), the international footballer who spent much of his career in the town, winning the Football Association Amateur Cup three times between 1955 and 1957 and the Northern League seven times. Newton Cap Viaduct was purchased by Durham County Council in 1972 and converted into a recreational footpath. In 1993, after a public campaign led by the Civic Society, the council were persuaded to keep the viaduct, and it was redecked and repurposed to carry road traffic as part of the Toronto Bypass scheme. This was aimed at relieving traffic passing through the small mining village of Toronto on the north bank of the

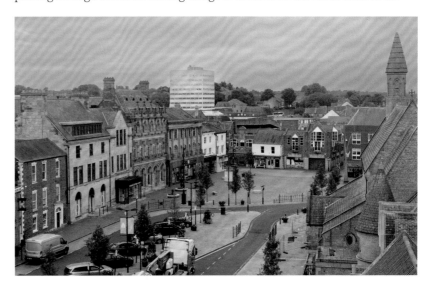

Figure 61
The former Department of Health and Social Security building, Vinovium House, dominating the skyline behind the buildings of the Market Place, viewed from the north-east.
[DP393009, Anna Bridson © Historic England Archive]

Wear and over the narrow and historic Newton Cap road bridge. The north end of the Bondgate tunnel was removed to make way for a short link road from Bob Hardisty Drive to the viaduct.

Around 1980 the stretch of Kingsway from Durham Chare to Durham Road was built, cutting through the long, narrow plots on the south side of the market place, and bisecting the medieval routeway of Durham Chare and Castle Chare. The development involved the loss of buildings along Durham Chare, Gaunless Terrace and outbuildings and extensions at the rear of properties on the south side of the market place, and it exposed the often unsightly backs of buildings never intended to be so visible. At around the same time, Princes Street was widened and reopened, resulting in the loss of the former Waterloo Hotel, better known as Rossi's ice-cream parlour.

In 1986 the railway station was replaced with a much smaller structure, which is now served by Northern Trains' Tees Valley Line and the Bishop Line Community Rail Partnership. The Bishop Line follows part of the original route of the Stockton and Darlington Railway. The Weardale Railway – a heritage railway between Bishop Auckland and Stanhope – runs from a separate platform, Bishop Auckland West. The former Spennymoor and Ferryhill line is now a popular walking and cycling route known as the Auckland Way Railway Path and the Durham line from the former railway viaduct northwards is a nine-mile walking route called the Brandon to Bishop Auckland Railway Path.

Shopping centres and supermarkets

From the late 20th century, commercial activity in the town began to change. In the 1980s many shops faced closure as they were hit by financial recession and rising costs; this decade saw Doggarts department store on Market Place and Newgate Street closed after over 100 years of trading. In 1983, to combat the decline in the local economy, the Newgate Shopping Centre was built next to the bus station, combining a range of new shops with a large multistorey car park. The aim was to attract shoppers to Bishop Auckland arriving either by car or by public transport. The sandstone elevation on Newgate Street is used to good effect, incorporating carved stone crests of the Bishops of Durham and Bishop Barrington recovered from the Barrington School in the market place. While the huge mass of the building overlaid the older street pattern and took activity away from some historic streets, its design played with castle-like architecture by using panelled brickwork, corbelling, buttresses and jettied first floors. The rise of supermarkets also changed the way people used the high street: Hintons, at no. 42 Market Place, was built in the 1970s (Fig. 62). To the south of the town, the former goods station site on the western side of Newgate Street (formerly South Road) and the former Robert Wilson & Sons site located along the western side of South Church Road were both redeveloped with supermarkets in 1987 and 2002 respectively.

The local economy of Bishop Auckland has been in a state of constant flux since the early 20th century and this has certainly shaped the way the town is experienced today. It is reassuring that despite the many changes, some of the high-street chains remain, and while many have left, this opens up fresh opportunities for a new era in which smaller businesses might thrive.

Figure 62
The former Hinton's supermarket, the dark brick building in the centre of the image, located at no. 42 Market Place dominating some of the smaller shops along Newgate Street.
[DP290653, Alun Bull © Historic England Archive]

7

Conservation and change

Bishop Auckland's rich past and its status as the largest town in southern County Durham have given it opportunities that smaller, less distinctive towns in need might not have had during the late 20th and early 21st centuries (*see* facing page). The approach to replanning the town centre from the late 1970s was quite a comprehensive one, and it is likely that much below-ground archaeological evidence was lost. Nonetheless, various measures to protect the town's heritage were employed to steady and guide the way forward, a process which had begun as early as 1952 when some of the town's most important buildings were listed. The Bishop Auckland Conservation Area was designated in 1969, then enlarged in 1990 and again in 1993. There were new listings in 1972, in the 1990s and again more recently, creating more than 80 listed buildings by the present day across the town centre, castle and park. The park itself was designated a grade II* Registered Park and Garden in 1986. In the 1980s, the Sun Inn on High Bondgate experienced 'heritage protection' of a very different order: rather than being demolished, it was dismantled and rebuilt some 18 miles (30km) away at Beamish, the Living Museum of the North.

Shopping and leisure became Bishop Auckland's firm economic basis in the late 20th century, reflected in town-centre development; it served extensive new areas of housing to the south of the settlement as well as tucked in around the town, such as off Durham Chare. The Newgate Shopping Centre of 1983 anchored an increasingly buoyant retail core in and around Newgate Street's well-established 19th-century shops and banks, which was soon brimming with shoppers (Fig. 63). Some new architecture was insensitive to local character: several plain blocks of shops were added along Newgate Street, while no. 42 and no. 43 Market Place (supermarkets from the 1970s and 1990s respectively) did not live up to the status of their prominent locations (*see* Fig. 62). Another anonymous-looking store replaced the Odeon cinema on Tenters Street in 1994–5; luckily, the former Hippodrome Picture House on Railway Street survived as a bingo hall, as did Newgate Street's former King's Hall Picture House for shops (*see* Fig. 76), although much altered. After closure in 1993, Newgate Street's former Wesleyan Methodist church became a community hub called the Four Clocks Centre, an imaginative and popular reuse of a prominent local landmark.

The same year, after district council offices had moved out to Crook, Bishop Auckland's grade II*-listed town hall was rescued and reborn as a cultural hub for the wider area. Hotels and inns had dominated this part of town since the

West Mural Tower, Silver Street, beautifully conserved by The Auckland Project with a grant from Historic England as part of the Heritage Action Zone. [DP248702, James O Davies © Historic England Archive]

Figure 63
The impact of the colossal Newgate Shopping Centre on
the town centre is best appreciated from the air.
[34095_008, Emma Trevarthen, 2018,
© Historic England Archive]

19th century and market places are traditionally favoured for socialising as well as trading. Indeed, by the 1990s, the pubs and bars here were still the place to relieve the pressure of the working week for revellers from across Wear valley and further afield, briefly earning the town the heady nickname of 'Bish Vegas'. This period of audacious nightlife showed the potential for animation that the large and distinctive market place still had, despite all but losing its primary role for market trading. The town's war memorial was moved here in 1986, and after a Townscape Heritage Initiative grant from the National Lottery Heritage Fund

(NLHF) saw some improvements from 1997, Durham County Council then funded major improvements to layout, paving and greenery in the early 21st century (Fig. 64). Together with a few restored shopfronts on Fore Bondgate, the market place started to reveal its potential as a revived public heart to the town.

Yet Bishop Auckland's late 20th-century energy led to a narrow, precarious economy unable to sustain the town centre in the face of the profound changes of the early 21st century. After the global economic downturn of 2008, Britain's high streets suffered a severe decline made worse by the rise of online shopping, the burden of high-street rent and rates, and competition from out-of-town retail parks, such as that at Tindale Crescent south of Bishop Auckland town centre. Many major retailers moved out from the town centre in the 2010s, including Marks & Spencer, Dorothy Perkins and Burton's, which had occupied the same building at no. 47 Newgate Street since the 1920s (*see* Fig. 75). Others closed altogether; the local family department store, Doggarts, shut in 1980, and Beales – the former Co-operative Stores at no. 80 Newgate Street – followed suit in 2017, leaving the town's second-largest listed building group vacant.

Newgate Street and the Bondgates were emptying out (Figs 65 and 66). Poor condition and vacancy affected many buildings here, with upper floors,

Figure 64
Townscape improvements to the market place began in the late 20th century, including moving the town's war memorial here from near the railway station in 1986.
[DP234517, Alun Bull © Historic England Archive]

Figure 65
Market filling station on North Bondgate boarded up in 1982.
[Image courtesy of The Northern Echo]

Figure 66
The rich collection of 19th-century buildings at the north end of Newgate Street became empty and fell into disrepair as prospects for Britain's high streets changed. This photograph was taken in 2019, just before the Covid-19 pandemic.
[Clare Howard © Historic England]

back rooms and rear yards falling into disrepair, some having been neglected since the mid-20th century. Many buildings had been too casually altered during the retail boom, especially with modern shopfronts, and the streetscape was looking tired. No. 11 Newgate Street partially collapsed in 2011 to leave a gap, echoed by cleared plots and derelict land on North Bondgate and Kingsway. Nearby, the disused King James I Grammar School was attacked by arsonists in 2007, leaving it in a parlous state alongside its neighbour, the former St Anne's School (National School) of 1855, which was subsequently almost entirely cleared.

Meanwhile, the future of Auckland Castle was thrown into doubt when as early as 2001, and most recently in 2010, the Church Commissioners voted to sell the outstanding set of Baroque paintings by Francisco de Zurbarán (1598–1664) that had hung there since the mid-18th century. This was suspected locally to be a precursor to selling off the castle and park, creating what was seen as a period of great peril in the castle's thousand-year history. With a weakened town centre, Bishop Auckland's future was increasingly uncertain. In 2011 the town's conservation area joined the West Mural Tower on the national Heritage at Risk Register, followed in 2013 by the Church of St Anne due to the poor condition of its roof. The town's rich historic environment was at risk, a situation sharply at odds with the strength of pride local people felt about their town.

Bishop Auckland Civic Society was set up by local people to stand up for and celebrate the town's inheritance and to promote the best for its future. It was officially formed in 1989, but dedicated groups had led successful campaigns to save key landmark buildings from 1984, including the town hall. Civic and amenity societies have not had as high a profile in the north-east of England as other parts of the UK, yet the handful of societies that thrive in this region have shown the importance of an independent community voice for heritage in places like Bishop Auckland. The town's society has been a prominent advocate, finding a central role in the struggles and successes to make best use of the town's heritage assets. As well as trails, design awards and blue plaques – all typical of a civic society's work – it led the successful campaign to prevent demolition of the Newton Cap Viaduct, resulting in its powerful 11 arches being saved and converted from rail to road by 1993, thought to be the first such conversion of a historic rail bridge in England (*see* Fig. 25). In the early 2000s, the society was at the forefront of the high-profile campaign to keep the Zurbarán paintings at Auckland Castle. Emphasising the paintings' message of political, social, ethnic and religious tolerance, the society and other local voices had the foresight to see them as a talisman to inspire future investment in Bishop Auckland, and as rooted a part of the town's heritage as the castle in which they hung.

But during this worrying period at the turn of the millennium, influential people had been listening. By the start of the 2010s, Bishop Auckland began to turn a significant corner towards a brighter future, guided by an emerging broad partnership of local public, private and charitable interests, some arriving in town with new ideas and a fresh sense of purpose.

In 2012, Auckland Castle, its property, paintings and park, were acquired by the Auckland Castle Trust and Zurbarán Trust, operating as The Auckland Project (TAP). These new bodies are now delivering the bold vision of UK-based financier Jonathan Ruffer to place the castle at the heart of an international visitor destination to benefit the town. The most recent chapter in Bishop Auckland's story was now underway.

TAP has since embarked upon an ambitious long-term programme to invest in their buildings and land, initially supported by the National Lottery Heritage Fund. When scaffolding shrouds such outstanding historic buildings, the sense of anticipation is intense but the results do not disappoint. Auckland Castle, one of the best-preserved bishop's palaces in the country, has been beautifully conserved inside and out, re-opening in 2019 to tell the story of the Bishops of Durham in exciting new ways. The quality of the work at the castle demonstrates the strength of the partnership between TAP, Durham County Council and Historic England. A striking new extension will soon expand this into a museum exploring faith, beliefs and religion in Britain (Fig. 67).

TAP's vision goes well beyond the castle. North of the town, a huge new open-air amphitheatre hosts Kynren, a summer spectacular night show with a cast of hundreds and an audience of thousands. The Mining Art Gallery opened to great acclaim in 2017 in historic buildings in the market place, home to an extraordinary local collection of art depicting the lives and creativity of Durham's mining communities: the Gemini Collection of over 400 pictures, collected and donated by Robert McManners and Gillian Wales, co-founders of the gallery. Opposite, two large redundant buildings (a former bank and the former Barrington School) have become the UK's first gallery for Spanish art history, exploring the Zurbarán connection (*see* Fig. 57). The ruinous West Mural Tower was rescued and readied for a future use, removing it from the national Heritage at Risk Register as a result (*see* chapter facing page), the

Figure 67
TAP's new Faith Museum, opening in 2023, includes a striking new extension to the castle's Scotland Wing designed by Níall McLoughlin Architects.
[DP290670, Alun Bull © Historic England Archive]

Figure 68
Auckland Tower, the welcome building and observation tower completed in 2018, has become something of a symbol for the future of the town.
[DP371415, Alun Bull © Historic England Archive]

castle's clocktower and some of the grounds have been restored, and the enormous walled garden has begun to grow flowers, fruit and vegetables again. Central to these projects has been a connection with local volunteers and training people in skills needed for a renewed local economy. There is great potential to reinforce the virtually unbroken, centuries-old historical link between the castle, park and town that is still very legible and active today.

The most thrilling of TAP's projects, Auckland Tower, has become something of a symbol for the future. The 2018 timber-framed welcome building and observation tower, by Níall McLaughlin Architects, soars 95ft (29m) high to offer fascinating views of the town, castle and landscape beyond (Fig. 68). When approaching the town from Durham, Auckland Tower is as bold and meaningful on the skyline as the town hall, but without the imposition of Vinovium House, the multistorey tower block which itself implied a new era when built in 1969–71 (*see* Fig. 61). Spirited but careful new architecture, firmly grounded in an understanding of history and setting, and guided by sound urban design principles, has great potential to add to Bishop Auckland's special architectural legacy.

In 2014, Historic England joined this regeneration momentum. It brought the Historic Places Panel – a team of independent specialists – to town to offer expert opinion on Bishop Auckland's welcome new period of renewal. They recommended it be guided by the needs of local people, to be set out in a masterplan that tackled the challenge of adapting for the visitor economy, and ensuring the benefit was felt directly in the fabric of the historic town centre. Durham County Council, who had been prioritising conservation spending here since the 1990s, duly prepared a masterplan in 2019.

The County Council won Heritage Action Zone (HAZ) status for Bishop Auckland in 2018. Set up by Historic England, the HAZ was a five-year partnership to unlock the potential of the town centre's heritage using a series of targeted projects. Expertise and resources were injected to push regeneration forward using the historic environment for the benefit of local people and businesses. Several years of research by and for Historic England – on which this book is based – now provides knowledge and understanding for future development.

Seed funds from Historic England were matched by Durham County Council and added to by the private sector, helping to repair the best historic buildings in the worst condition. Grants to the owners of nos 10, 25 (listed grade II) and 47 Newgate Street are illustrative of the ambition so far. Plans for these former shops involve almost anything but the sale of high-street brands, showing that diversifying the town centre will be important to its survival (Fig. 69). Upper floors are gradually being put back to use, including as overnight accommodation for visitors. Though under-occupied and in need of attention, the town's historic commercial architecture is inspiring sound conservation and, alongside TAP's dynamism, the HAZ has begun to revitalise economic, social and cultural life.

Figure 69
*Unoccupied commercial buildings on Newgate Street,
Fore Bondgate and elsewhere will require diverse new
uses to secure their future. Nos 2–4 Newgate Street
have recently been transformed into the Fox's Tale Café.
[DP290676, Alun Bull © Historic England Archive]*

The coronavirus (Covid-19) outbreak from early 2020 had devastating consequences for this momentum. High-street and visitor economies so important to Bishop Auckland's revival took another big hit, knocking off track projects planned by players large and small. TAP's grand ambition to transform the market place for visitors has been set back, with the four historic pubs and other property they own there continuing to be mothballed and extending the negative effect of vacancy (Fig. 70). Rescuing the enormous former Co-operative Stores on Newgate Street is also proving difficult in the current economic climate. Funds to repair the roof of the Church of St Anne remain elusive, and solutions for Victoria Avenue's former Mechanics Institute and Temperance Hall are also proving stubborn. Even though HAZ work has shown their potential, they are fraught with high costs and ownership problems (*see* Fig. 39). The once-charred shell of the former King James I Grammar School on South Church Road shows the perils of long-term vacancy, but the front façade was saved when recently redeveloping it for housing by the Railway Housing Association.

Yet there have been some wonderful successes despite the setbacks. One surprisingly positive consequence of Covid has been a renewed interest in local green spaces, with the community relishing the rich, freely accessible resource of the historic park on their doorstep. TAP's landscape conservation plans should reinforce this experience. A plucky variety of small shops, cafés and galleries is growing on Fore Bondgate, Market Place and North Bondgate, exploiting historic character in order to thrive. The annual Food Festival pumps the market place full of life over a busy weekend each spring. Thus, the north end of town is

Figure 70
The collection of historic pubs on the north and west side of Market Place, including the former Castle Bar, the Queen's Head and the Post Chaise, helped to bring the open space to life. Reusing them now will remove the deadening effect that their mothballing has recently had on the market place.
[DP290673, Alun Bull © Historic England Archive]

Figure 71
The grade II-listed water fountain and its setting at the
meeting of Castle Chare and Durham Chare have been
conserved as part of the Heritage Action Zone.
[DP393062, Anna Bridson © Historic England Archive]

slowly re-establishing itself as a characterful spot to spend money and time relaxing. Even small projects bring optimism: two handsome Gothic public water fountains, on Castle Chare and High Bondgate, have been conserved, and King James I Academy is working on reusing its redundant outbuildings, listed grade II, for the community (Fig. 71).

The HAZ and TAP's work has unleashed the fascination local people have in stories from the past. Four annual heritage and history festivals have brought to life the trials, tales and trends of town life from Roman Binchester and Victorian baking powder to the pride of Bishop Auckland Football Club. Particularly successful in engaging young people, the festival should remain a mainstay of the town's calendar, supported by the Civic Society, Bishop Auckland People's Museum (who hope to open the Hippodrome's forgotten cinema auditorium), Durham Amateur Football Trust and others (Fig. 72; *see* Fig. 79). Research continues to shine a light on the town's history, including the quieter parts such as the industrial quarter south of Peel Street. Here, robust 19th-century buildings are ripe for regeneration to protect the town's increasingly rare industrial past (Fig. 73). The significance of some gems is only now coming to light, such as Gregory's on Newgate Street, a much-loved and surprisingly intact former high-street butcher's shop, now a baker's and deli, which became a grade II-listed building in 2020 (*see* Figs 46 and 77). A County Council project has seen local people nominate more than 80 buildings, sites and other features for a Local List, a way of celebrating and protecting parts of our built heritage special to the local community.

Intensive work by TAP and Durham University on the town's archaeological potential has started to reveal some of its buried secrets. Using geophysical survey techniques, excavation and other forms of research, earlier phases of the castle have been discovered below the surface (*see* Fig. 2). Importantly, new evidence – particularly that mapped from aerial sources – seems to confirm what earlier documentary research had concluded, that the park was once much larger than it is today, suggesting greater importance to land beyond that currently protected through designation (*see* Fig. 4). Also of particular interest archaeologically is land at Castle Chare, North Bondgate and The Batts, the latter providing a valued expanse of open space for public recreation and containing a trio of historically important bridges. The Bishop Big Dig project by Durham University and TAP has brought excavation to local people's doorsteps, with dozens of test pits being opened up in gardens, yards and public spaces. The excitement of local people has proven just as important to the town's heritage as the artefacts being found under their feet. All this work is addressing the agenda set by the North East Regional Research Framework for the Historic Environment (Fig. 74).

There is much to learn from surviving buildings, too. The HAZ's research suggests many pre-18th-century buildings were not totally demolished during later development, potentially leaving much older fabric in place for us to

Figure 72
Engagement with the local community has been a
strong part of the Heritage Action Zone, from heritage
tours to working with local students. Sixth-form
students from New College Durham were volunteer
stewards at the History Fair in 2022.
[Reproduced with permission from Andrew Heptinstall
Photography]

Figure 73
A local artist has enlivened the former industrial area
with legal graffiti as a way of remembering one much-
celebrated connection with the town's history.
[DP393088, Anna Bridson © Historic England
Archive]

Figure 74
There have been some fascinating artefacts discovered by the Bishop Big Dig during 2022.
[Reproduced with permission from Andrew Heptinstall Photography]

rediscover. The walls, cellars and roof voids of historic buildings could reveal much earlier remains, and even stone plot boundary walls can be revealing if properly 'read'.

Most recently, Durham County Council was successful in two further large bids to government, from the Future High Streets Fund (2020) and the Stronger Towns Fund (2021), inspired by its HAZ partnership with Historic England, and by TAP's growing programme. Major investment is due to follow, including in town-centre historic buildings as well as infrastructure planned in and out of town.

Bishop Auckland is in the throes of being remodelled and reborn as a characterful destination for relaxation, culture and heritage. TAP's Auckland Tower acts as a beacon for this transformation, while local entrepreneurs, with help from the HAZ, are busy bringing historic streets back to life around it. Bishop Auckland's rich legacy of historic buildings, landscape and archaeology is central to its future: a dramatic, characterful, sometimes challenging historic environment that was always more than just a market town, now being steered towards a bright new future that few could have predicted just 20 years ago. One of the strongest parts of the UK's economy is now the benefit drawn from giving visitors a warm welcome, whether from home or abroad, for an afternoon or for a summer holiday. Bishop Auckland is increasingly ready to join in this adventure.

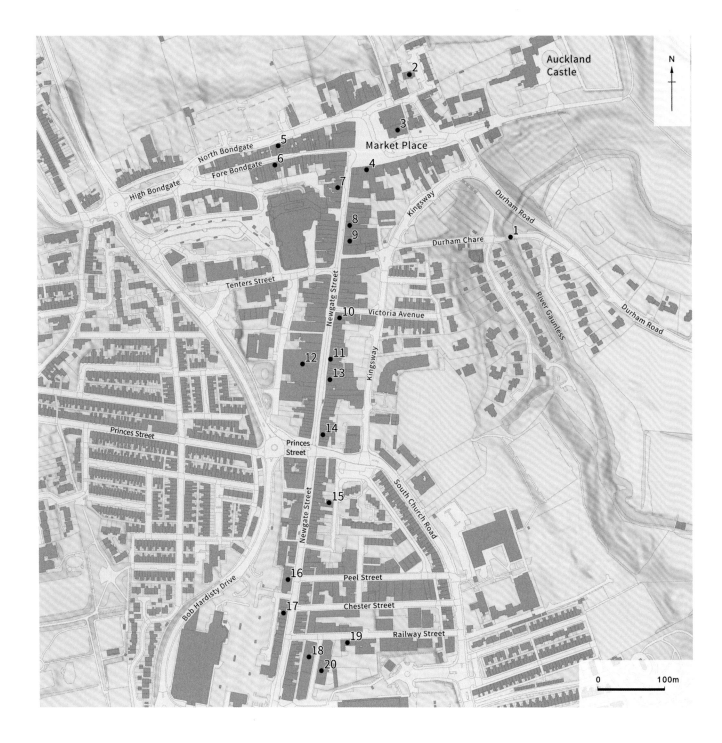

Gazeteer of selected sites within the town

The following map and gazetteer present a tour of the historic core of Bishop Auckland. They highlight some of the sites key to the town's history and development.

1 Gaunless Bridge, Durham Chare (and Castle Chare)

Before 1929, Durham Chare was the main route linking the market place at Bishop Auckland with Durham. The use of 'chare' suggests the route may be contemporary with that of the market place and the Bishop's Palace established in the 12th century. The footpath leading up the steep bank on the west side of the Gaunless Bridge is known as Castle Chare and provided direct access to the castle entrance. Today its south end is marked by a stone drinking fountain erected in 1873 by the Temperance Society; it was recently restored as part of the Heritage Action Zone.

The crossing of the Gaunless was certainly bridged by 1576 and by the mid-18th century the Bowes and Sunderland Bridge turnpike road followed this route. The earlier part of the bridge appears broadly 18th century in date, and it may have been built by the Turnpike Trust. It was widened in 1822.

2 The Elms, Market Place

The Elms has the hallmarks of a large mid-18th-century house with its narrow handmade bricks, tall sash windows and central door with patterned overlight (*see* Figs 20 and 21). However, scars within its external fabric, particularly on its east elevation (facing the castle), suggest that it has undergone a number of changes and the building may have earlier origins.

In the early 19th century the building was used as Mrs Dobson's School for Young Ladies, and by the late 19th century it was occupied by Doctor Valentine Hutchinson, who lived here with his family and held surgeries in the former study/library. The building was used as the Wear Valley council offices in the late 20th century and is now private flats. Many of its original internal features are thought to survive.

3 Church of St Anne (and Market Place)

The earliest reference to a church on this site, built as a chapel of ease to reduce overcrowding at the Bishop's Palace chapel, dates to 1391 when the bishop granted land to extend the churchyard. This medieval church was rebuilt in 1781 and this was in turn rebuilt as the present church in 1846–8. The construction of the present church was designed by the local architect William Thompson (of the well-known Thompson family of architects). The church, in its neo-Gothic Early English style, remains a striking feature at the heart of the historic market place (*see* Figs 35 and 36).

4 Auckland House, Market Place (formerly Hedley's and later Doggarts)

Auckland House, which was built as a large drapery emporium in the mid-19th century, was extended and refronted with its grand classical features in about 1871 for Robert Hedley at a cost of £10,000 (*see* Fig. 41). The interior rooms were largely open-plan with ample space for multiple counters on the ground floor, showrooms on the first floor and warehousing on the second floor. The store was taken over by Arthur Doggart in the later decades of the 19th century and grew to become a well-known department store with branches across the north-east of England.

5 No. 17 North Bondgate

No. 17 North Bondgate is one of the earliest buildings in the Bondgate area – although many more may conceal earlier fabric – dating to the early 18th century as suggested by its steeply pitched roof and its narrow handmade bricks (*see* Fig. 22).

Buildings with similar characteristics include nos 55–57 Fore Bondgate and no. 47 Market Place (now part of the Miners Art Gallery). The eastern gable of no. 17 North Bondgate also contains the remnants of a shorter gable end wall; the rest of this neighbouring building has been demolished.

The practice of retaining what would have been the shared party wall between two buildings was common in Bishop Auckland and these can be spotted sandwiched between buildings or up against exposed gable ends throughout the town.

6 Nos 10–11 Fore Bondgate (formerly Shepherd's Inn)

These two properties were probably built as one large building (one of the largest in the town) in the 18th century, with extensive gardens to the rear (*see* Fig. 18). It was probably used as the town's public assembly rooms. By 1875 the building had been subdivided into a private house on one side and a public house on the other. The latter included two large assembly rooms known as the 'commercial room' and the 'long room', which were used to accommodate the local magistrates' courts and other town meetings before the town hall was constructed in 1862.

7 Row of former hotels and banks, Newgate Street

This row of buildings was rebuilt incrementally between 1898 and 1912 as part of the widening of Newgate Street to accommodate increased traffic within the town (*see* Fig. 47). The buildings share similar characteristics such as parapets on top of the elevations and keystones set within window lintels. Interestingly, nos 10 and 18 were built as banks and are faced with stone, whereas the others are of red brick and accommodated public houses and hotels, including the White Lion, the Criterion and the Market Tavern.

8 No. 21 Newgate Street (formerly York City and County Bank)

The HSBC building with its red-brick façade was built in 1893 and altered in 1901 (as commemorated by the date of the rainwater pipe heads) to the designs of Walter H. Brierley and James Demaine of York. It was described in 1893 as containing a banking room, strong room, manager's room and lock-up shop with three large offices at first-floor level and retiring rooms and stores in the basement.

9 No. 25 Newgate Street (formerly McIntyre's)

This building was constructed in the early 19th century as two separate buildings. They were occupied at various times by small independent tradesmen including a shoemaker, saddler and a hairdresser, perhaps with retail space at ground level, domestic accommodation above and workshops to the rear. The two properties were amalgamated in about 1891, shortly before McIntyre's boot, shoe and leather goods manufacturers took over the premises, a position which they held for over 100 years (*see* Fig. 51).

The interesting 1930s Art Nouveau shopfront, with its recessed lobbies, curved sheet glass and high-quality materials, including polished granite and bronze plating, is an important survival.

10 No. 47 Newgate Street (formerly Cleminson's shop and later Burton's)

No. 47 Newgate Street, formerly Victoria House, was constructed in the early 1870s as part of the establishment of the new street, Victoria Avenue (Fig. 75). It was built for Mr Isiah Cleminson and was described in 1891 as a 'colossal cabinet and furniture emporium' of four storeys containing 'palatial rooms', 'extensive cellarage' and a lift. It was transformed into a Burton's tailors shop in about 1923. Burton's and Dorothy Perkins occupied the premises until 2009.

11 No. 69 Newgate Street

This building – with its steeply pitched roof and low elevation – has the hallmarks of a building pre-dating the 19th century (*see*

Figure 75
Victoria House at the corner of Victoria Avenue was built as Cleminson's furniture emporium in the 1870s. It became Burton's tailors in the 1920s. [DP393020, Anna Bridson © Historic England Archive]

Fig. 7). Hidden fabric such as timber framing and the roof structure might provide further clues as to its origins.

12 No. 80 Newgate Street (formerly the Co-operative Stores)

The Bishop Auckland Co-operative Society established its first independent premises on this site in 1862. The building was replaced by a new, purpose-built shop in 1873. The shop was extended in 1882–3 and 1892–4, and in 1902 they also acquired the neighbouring premises (originally built in 1894). The architects of the two earlier phases were William Vickers Thompson and his brother Robert Wilkinson Thompson, of the well-established Thompson family of architects based in Bishop Auckland.

The four phases of development can be identified in the front elevation by the date stones on the parapet and by the cleverly disguised vertical straight joints (*see* Fig. 44). The front part of the building provided the retail space composed of multiple departments, while the rear incorporated offices, warehouse buildings, stabling and processing and manufacturing buildings.

13 No. 77 Newgate Street (formerly King's Hall Picture House)

The King's Hall Picture House was built in 1914 for G. W. Rudd to the design of local architect Douglas Crawford (Fig. 76). It comprised a ground-floor arcade of shops which led to the picture hall at the rear. The establishment soon expanded into the neighbouring premises (nos 73 and 75, formerly known as Beethoven House) and by 1937 it was advertised as the King's Lending Library with ballroom and restaurant. The King's originally had three storeys and was probably reduced in height as part of its transformation into a supermarket in 1962.

Figure 76
The King's Hall Picture House on Newgate Street was established in 1914. The ground floor became a supermarket in the 1960s.
[DP393022, Anna Bridson © Historic England Archive]

14 Nos 103–105 Newgate Street (Gregory's)

Gregory's and the building to the left of it were probably built in the mid-19th century as a pair of houses with two rooms on each floor (*see* Figs 43 and 46). William Gregory, butcher, occupied one of the two premises in 1871, with the butcher's shop at the front and living accommodation for him and his family above. By 1881 the family business also occupied the adjacent building, creating a double frontage. Plans of the building drafted in 1903 suggest that there was a pork shop on the left, a beef shop on the right (each with separate central entrances as seen today), and a kitchen and sitting room to the rear. A series of outbuildings were arranged around a rear yard containing a slaughterhouse and boiling house (for boiling fat to make tallow for candles and soap).

As well as its colourful stained-glass windows (dating from about 1910), the interior of the shop retains tiles depicting country scenes with cows and pigs, and steel rails attached to the ceiling for the easy manoeuvring of meat around the shop – these are rare and important features (Fig. 77).

15 Former back-to-back cottages, South Terrace

In the first half of the 19th century back-to-back cottages were erected on South Terrace and the east side of Newgate Street (formerly South Road). These would have been very small, probably with a single room to the ground and first floor (Fig. 78). The occupants would have had access to shared washing and toilet facilities in a

Figure 77
Gregory's retains some of its stained glass dating from about 1910, due to be repaired at the time of writing.
[DP290666, Alun Bull © Historic England Archive]

communal yard to the rear. They were made into through-housing (where two back-to-back houses were knocked though to create a larger house) by the end of the 19th century, probably as a result of interventions by the Local Board of Health to improve the living conditions of the town's poorest residents.

Figure 78
A pair of former back-to-back houses on South Terrace.
[DP393073, Anna Bridson © Historic England Archive]

16 Wesleyan Methodists Church (Four Clocks Centre)

The Wesleyan Methodist Church was established between 1908 and 1914, overlooking the former Railway Goods Station complex to the west (*see* Fig. 37). The church was designed by London-based architects Henry Thomas Gordon and Josiah Gunter, and constructed by builder Thomas Hilton. Built in a neo-Gothic style in rock-faced stone with ashlar dressings, it is a prominent landmark in this part of Bishop Auckland.

17 Brougham Place, Newgate Street (formerly South Road)

Brougham Place was built in the early 1830s as a row of single-storey houses. The 1851 census listed 37 separate properties within the row. The occupants were mainly colliery workers. The northern section was demolished in the early 20th century and replaced with the Wesleyan Methodist Church. A stone plaque on the wall of the Four Clocks Centre (former Wesleyan Methodist Church) preserves the name 'Brougham Place 1835'.

Figure 79
The Hippodrome Theatre on Railway Street, later a picture house, built in 1909.
[DP393071, Anna Bridson © Historic England Archive]

18 No. 27 Railway Street (former Hippodrome Cinema)

The former Hippodrome Cinema, now a bingo hall, opened on 30 November 1909 and was designed by Darlington architect Joseph James Taylor (under the supervision of George F. Ward of Birmingham-based architectural firm Owen and Ward) for Signor Rino Pepi, a theatre impresario who created a chain of music halls across northern England (Fig. 79). It was renamed the Hippodrome Picture House in the early 20th century. It was converted to a bingo hall in the early 1960s. It has a central

auditorium beyond the main entrance foyer to Railway Street.

19 Auckland Engine Works

The arrival of the railways in the 1840s and 1850s brought new industries to Bishop Auckland. The Lingford Gardiner & Co engineering works were established in the late 1850s on a plot of land between Chester Street and Railway Street, close to the Railway Station and well positioned to connect to the railway network (*see* Figs 30 and 33). The works closed in 1931, and by the mid-20th century the buildings across the site had been repurposed as a timber yard, drill hall, mission hall and instruction centre for boys.

20 Former Drill Hall, Union Street

A drill hall was established in the former Lingford Gardiner & Co buildings in the early 1900s. The hall is a single-storey brick building with arch-headed windows, and pier and panel brickwork with dog-tooth dentils. On 9 October 1906, Prince Francis of Teck (brother of Mary of Teck, who in 1910 became queen consort to her husband King George V) attended the opening of a three-day military bazaar of the 2nd Volunteer Battalion, Durham Light Infantry, held at the drill hall.

Notes

1 Reports can be found on the Historic England Research Reports Series database, via the Historic England web page: https://historicengland.org.uk/research/results/reports/.

2 Durham County Council Historic Environment Record no. H3290 (flint artefact from the park).

3 Durham County Council Historic Environment Record no. H1416, cremation urn found in 1757 near Bishop Trevor's bridge over the River Gaunless in Auckland Castle Park; National Record Historic Environment monument UID 24247, Roman cemetery in Auckland Castle Park.

4 Greenwell 1852.

5 Greenwell 1857, 33–41.

6 Kirby 1971, 15.

7 Durham University Library MSP 91 f4: pen and ink elevation of the outward court walls and gateway of Auckland castle by John Langstaffe, 1665.

8 Mackenzie 1827, 163.

9 Durham Record Office EP/Au.SA 11/52: Grant of the school house, lately built near to the ruined chapel of St. Anne in the town of Bishop Auckland, with the adjoining cottage, 1638; Raine 1852, 99.

10 *The Daily News*, 25 January 1925, 11.

11 Toulmin Smith 1907, 70.

12 Durham Record Office UD/BA 432/761: Building application for Queen's Head Hotel, 1898.

13 Kirby 1971, 15.

14 Durham University Library MSP 91 f1: Pencil drawing of a 'draught' elevation of the east end of Auckland castle chapel with a tablet to Bishop John Cosin.

15 The College of Arms MS C.41: 'Durham Church notes' fol. 10b Prospect of the Castle, Chapel and Town of Bishop Auckland, 1666.

16 Durham County Record Office PA HL/PO/PU/1/1747/21G2: Public Act, 21 George II, c. 5 Act for repairing the road between Bowes and Sunderland Bridge, 1747.

17 King 1980, 49.

18 Durham County Record Office EP/Au.San 2/13: Order of service for the commemoration of the centenary of St. Anne's church, 22 February 1948.

19 *Ibid.*

20 Census for England and Wales 1851, Bishop Auckland, District 11c, page 49.

21 Census for England and Wales 1871, Bishop Auckland, District 2, page 4; *The Durham County Advertiser*, 14 May 1875, 5.

22 Census for England and Wales 1901, Bishop Auckland, District 2, page 10.

23 Durham Record Office D/Loco 1/1/1: Act of Parliament for Bishop Auckland and Weardale Railway (1 Victoria, c.cxxii), 15 July 1837.

24 *The Durham County Advertiser*, 3 April 1857.

25 Durham University Library CCB MP 511: Plan of Property at Bishop Auckland, Proposed to be divided into Building Ground', by Henry Tuke, 1856.

26 Durham Record Office UD/BA 432/99: Building application for the extension of Lingford Gardiner's works in Railway Street and Chester Street, 1868.

27 Whellan 1894, 343.

28 Rickards 1836, 130

29 *The Durham Chronicle*, 31 October 1862, 8; *The Builder*, 7 April 1860, 216–17.

30 *Newcastle Daily Chronicle*, 15 May 1912, 8.

31 *The Northern Echo*, 16 June 1875, 4; Durham Record Office UD/BA 432/312: Building application for Temperance Hall, 1875; *South Durham and Cleveland Mercury*, 20 January 1877, 6.

32 Durham Record Office D/X 1131/2: *The Auckland Times and Herald*, 1881.

33 Durham Record Office UD/BA 434: Bishop Auckland Building Control Indexes 1868–1948; Kelly 1914, 21; Durham Record Office UD/BA 432/517: Building application for Young Men's Church Institute, 1881.

34 *Daily Gazette for Middlesbrough*, 14 April 1893, 2; Durham Record Office UD/BA 434/765: Plans of Yorkshire Penny Bank, 1898.

35 Durham Record Office UD/BA 432/309: Plans of the York City and County Bank, 1891.

36 Durham Record Office UD/BA 432/538: Co-operative Stores, Bishop Auckland, 1882; Durham Record Office UD/BA 432/538: Co-operative Stores, Bishop Auckland, 1882; Readshaw 1910, 157.

37 *The Northern Echo*, 5 July 1875, 1; Durham Record Office UD/BA 432/114: Building application for Auckland House (Doggarts), 1871.

38 Durham Record Office UD/BA 434/676: Plans for shops and public houses, Newgate Street, 1877.

39 Durham Record Office UD/BA 432/761: Building application for Queen's Head Hotel, 1898; Durham Record Office UD/BA 432/1186: Building application for the Bay Horse Hotel, 1909.

40 Durham Record Office UD/BA plan no. 1397: Building application for alterations to White Lion, 1911; Kelly 1914, 27; *Newcastle Journal*, 10 May 1911, 5. The White Lion was listed in White's Directory of 1827.

41 Durham Record Office UD/BA 432/965: Building application for proposed Cricket Pavilion, 1903.

42 Morrison 2015, 161.

43 *Kinematograph Weekly*, 6 January 1921, 205.

44 Durham Record Office DRO UD/BA 432/1358 and 1361: Building application for proposed Picture House Arcade, 1914.

45 *The North-Eastern Daily Gazette*, 3 December 1909, 4.

46 *The Yorkshire Post*, Monday 30 December 1929; *The Yorkshire Post*, Monday 6 January 1930.

47 Roberts *et al* 2021, 144.

48 Bishop Auckland Urban District Council 1954, 14–17.

References and further reading

Alastair Coey Architects 2019 'Former Bishop Auckland Mechanics' Institute, 27 Victoria Avenue, Bishop Auckland: Historic Building Report'. *Historic England Research Report Series*, 30-2019

Alastair Coey Architects 2019 'Former Central Stores to Bishop Auckland Co-operative Society, 80 Newgate Street, Bishop Auckland: Historic Building Report'. *Historic England Research Report Series*, 16-2019

Alastair Coey Architects 2019 'Former McIntyre's Shoe Shop, 25 Newgate Street, Bishop Auckland'. *Historic England Research Report Series*, 29-2019

Barfoot, P., and Wilkes, J. 1791 *The Universal British Directory of Trade, Commerce and Manufacture*, vols 1–5. London

Bishop Auckland Urban District Council 1954 *The Urban District of Bishop Auckland: Official Guide*. London: Suburban and Provincial Association

Bishop Auckland Urban District Council 1969 *Bishop Auckland, County Durham, Official Guide and Industrial Handbook*. Cheltenham and London

Cockerill, K. 2005 *Bridges of the River Wear*. Seaham: The People's History

Cox, T. 1738 *Magna Britannia antiqua and nova: or, A new, exact, and comprehensive survey of the ancient and present state of Great Britain*. London

Durham County Council 2014 'Heritage, Landscape and Design: Bishop Auckland Conservation Area Appraisal'. Durham: Durham County Council Heritage, Landscape and Design

Fair, P. 1820 *A Description of Bishop Auckland, including the castle and park, and several gentlemen's seats in the neighbourhood; together with a brief account of the Bishops of Durham since the Restoration*. Bishop Auckland

Fordyce, W. 1855 *The History and Antiquities of the County Palatine of Durham* Durham

Green, A. 2016 *Building for England: John Cosin's Architecture in Renaissance Durham and Cambridge*. Durham Medieval and Renaissance Monographs and Essays 4. Durham.

Greenwell, W. (ed) 1852 *Boldon Buke: a survey of the possessions of the see of Durham made by order of Bishop Hugh Pudsey in 1183, with a translation*. Publications of the Surtees Society, vol 25

Greenwell, W. (ed) 1857 *Bishop Hatfield's Survey: A Record of the Possessions of the See of Durham*. Publications of the Surtees Society, vol 32

Howard, C., Pullen, R., and Rimmer, J. 2021 'Bishop Auckland, County Durham: Historic Area Assessment'. *Historic England Research Report Series*, 22-2021

Hutchinson, T. 2005 *The History of Bishop Auckland*. Sunderland

Hutchinson, T. 2009 *Bishop Auckland: A Century of Postcards*. Newcastle

Hutchinson, T. 2011 *Newton Cap and Toronto: Two Communities by the River Wear*. Newcastle

Hutchinson, T. 2012 *Bishop Auckland Past Times*. Newcastle

Hutchinson, T. 2015 *Bishop Auckland Past and Present*. Newcastle

Hutchinson, T. 2018 *Bishop Auckland and District*. Newcastle

Hutchinson, W. 1823 *The History and Antiquities of the County Palatine of Durham*, vol III. Durham: G Wallier

Jecock, M. 2021 'The Road, Rail and Parkland Bridges of Bishop Auckland, Co Durham: An Assessment of the Historical and Archaeological Evidence'. *Historic England Research Report Series*, 4-2021

Hagar and Company 1851 *Hagar and Company's Directory of the County of Durham*. Nottingham

Kelly 1914 *Kelly's Directory of Durham*. London: Kelly's Directories Limited

King, R. W. 1980 'Joseph Spence of Byfleet, Part III.' *Garden History*, 8(2) Summer 1980, 44–65

Kirby, D. A. (ed) 1971 *Parliamentary Surveys of the Bishopric of Durham*. Vol I. Publications of the Surtees Society, vol 183. Gateshead

Laurie, B. 1995 *Bishop Auckland in Wartime*. Bishop Auckland and Sedgefield

Laurie, B. 1998 *Bishop Auckland in the 1950s*. Bishop Auckland and Sedgefield

Laurie, B. 2001 *The Changing Face of Bishop Auckland*. Bishop Auckland and Newton Aycliffe

Laurie, B. nd *The Listed Bridges of Bishop Auckland*. Durham

Longstaff, J. R. 1994 *The First Hundred Years of Bishop Auckland Golf Club 1894–1994*. Bishop Auckland: Bishop Auckland Golf Club

Mackenzie, E. 1827 *A Descriptive and Historical Account of the Town & County of Newcastle-upon-Tyne, Including the Borough of Gateshead*. Newcastle upon Tyne: MacKenzie & Dent

MacKenzie, E., and Ross, M. 1834 *An Historical, Topographical and Descriptive View of the County Palatine of Durham*, vol II. Newcastle

Morrison, K. A. 2015 *Woolworth's: 100 Years on the High Street*. Swindon: Historic England

Raine, Revd J. 1852 *A Brief Historical Account of the Episcopal Castle, or Palace, of Auckland. Completed from Records in the Auditor's Office at Durham and Other Authorities*. Durham

Readshaw, T. 1910 *The Bishop Auckland Industrial Co-operative Flour and Provision Society Ltd Jubilee History 1860–1910*. Manchester

Rennison, R. W. 1998 'Richard Cail (1812–1893): Victorian contractor and man of many parts.' *Transactions of the Newcomen Society*, 70(1), 161–83

Richley, M. 1872 *History and characteristics of Bishop Auckland: including a description of the parish church of St. Andrew's Auckland, St. Ann's Chapel, the Bishop's Palace, and other places of historic interest in the neighbourhood...: embellished with steel engravings, facsimiles of the parish registers &c*. Bishop Auckland

Rickards, G. K. 1836 *The Statutes of the United Kingdom of Great Britain and Ireland* [1807–1868/69], volume 76. London: His Majesty's statute and law printers

Roberts, M., Pevsner, N., and Williamson, E. 2021 *The Buildings of England: County Durham*. New edition. London: Yale University Press

Rollason, D. (ed) 2017 *Princes of the Church: Bishops and their Palaces*. Society for Medieval Archaeology Monograph 39. London: Routledge

Slack, G. 2015 *Bishop Auckland and the Railways*. Published for Bishop Auckland Station History Group, County Durham

Slack, G. 2016 *Lingford Gardiner & Co. 'a brief history'*. Published for Bishop Auckland Station History Group, County Durham

The British Directory Office 1790 *The Universal British Directory of Trade, Commerce, and Manufacture*, vol II. London

Toulmin Smith, L. 1907 *The Itinerary of John Leland in About the Years 1535–43*. London: G Bell

Whellan, F. and Company 1894 *History, Topography and Directory of the County Palatine of Durham*. London

Informed Conservation Series

This popular Historic England series highlights the special character of some of our most important historic areas and the development of the pressures they are facing. There are over 30 titles in the series, some of which look at whole towns such as Bridport, Coventry and Margate or distinctive urban districts, such as the Jewellery Quarter in Birmingham and Ancoats in Manchester, while others focus on particular building types in a particular place. A few are national in scope focusing, for example, on English school buildings and garden cities.

The purpose of the series is to raise awareness of the interest and importance of aspects of the built heritage of towns and cities undergoing rapid change or large-scale regeneration. A particular feature of each book is a final chapter that focuses on conservation issues, identifying good examples of the re-use of historic buildings and highlighting those assets or areas for which significant challenges remain.

As accessible distillations of more in-depth research, they also provide a useful resource for heritage professionals tackling, as many of the books do, places and building types that have not previously been subjected to investigation from the historic environment perspective. As well as providing a lively and informed discussion of each subject, the books also act as advocacy documents for Historic England and its partners in protecting historic places and keeping them alive for current and future generations.

More information on each of the books in the series and on forthcoming titles can be found on the Historic England website.

HistoricEngland.org.uk